# WATCH THE BEAR

## A Half Century with the Brown Bears of Alaska

**DEREK STONOROV**

University of Nebraska Press

LINCOLN

Excerpts of chapter 28 were previously published in *Living in Harmony with Bears* (Alaska: National Audubon Society, 2000), 11–12.

The University of Nebraska Press is part of a land-grant institution with campuses and programs on the past, present, and future homelands of the Pawnee, Ponca, Otoe-Missouria, Omaha, Dakota, Lakota, Kaw, Cheyenne, and Arapaho Peoples, as well as those of the relocated Ho-Chunk, Sac and Fox, and Iowa Peoples.

Names: Stonorov, Derek, author.
Title: Watch the bear : a half century with the brown bears of Alaska / Derek Stonorov.
Description: Lincoln : University of Nebraska Press, [2023]
Identifiers: LCCN 2022031538
ISBN 9781496233431 (paperback)
ISBN 9781496234957 (epub)
ISBN 9781496234964 (pdf)
Subjects: LCSH: Brown bear—Alaska. | Brown bear—Behavior—Alaska. | BISAC: NATURE / Animals / Bears | HISTORY / United States / State & Local / West (AK, CA, CO, HI, ID, MT, NV, UT, WY)
Classification: LCC QL737.C27 S7295 2023 |
DDC 599.78409798—dc23/eng/20220712
LC record available at https://lccn.loc.gov/2022031538

Set in Arno Pro by Mikala R. Kolander.

*For Molly*

# CONTENTS

# ILLUSTRATIONS

**Map**

**Photographs**

*Following page 92*

# ACKNOWLEDGMENTS

Without the suggestions, critiquing, and editing by my wife, Molly, this book never would have been completed.

The old adage "you meet your friends along the trail" is more than true. I met Madeleine Eno completely by chance after writing a first draft for this book. As my patient and more than competent first editor, her wise advice on organization and style helped bring *Watch the Bear* into a publishable manuscript. Eventually, we did walk the same trails on Tutuk Creek. Madeleine is a true gem and is not scared of bears.

John and Mary Beth Schoen have long encouraged my writing efforts. Having a knowledgeable person like Mary Beth say "I really learned about bear behavior" after she read the manuscript pushed me toward seeking publication. The story, science, and conclusions are my own, but having the support, advice, and eventual manuscript review by John, a respected wildlife ecologist, editor, and accomplished author, has been a great gift.

Nancy Lord's comments after reviewing *Watch the Bear* confirmed to me that I had both a good story and the ability to interpret the intricacies of bear behavior. Confirmation is very important to aspiring writers. I've never watched bears with Nancy, although one snowy spring day we searched for dens. Bears have a true friend in Nancy, as do belugas, salmon, and other living things.

Clark Whitehorn at Bison Books and the University of Nebraska Press has been supportive from query to publication. His interest and knowledge of bears and their behavior along with his enthusiasm make me grateful to Clark for allowing me to tell my story.

Most of the information about the movement of bears from one place to another in *Watch the Bear* is my own. However, the research and publications of Lee Glen, Lee Miller, Jim Faro, Dick Sellers, and Sean Farley of the Alaska Department of Fish and Game, as well as Grant Hilderbrand of the National Park Service and Karyn Rode of the U.S. Geological Survey, have undoubtedly influenced me and certainly added greatly to my knowledge of bears.

Al Stokes is long gone but his teaching still enters most of my thoughts on behavior. He's constantly peering over my shoulder asking, "How do you know that?" Much of the data I collected with him appears in this book.

Jane Kauvar, John Athens, and Michael Gill read the manuscript and offered encouragement.

Lastly and most importantly, I am indebted to Ken and Chris Day and Dave Bachrach for sharing their experiences, knowledge, and friendship. Perhaps without knowing, they are among the most important contributors to this book.

# WATCH THE BEAR

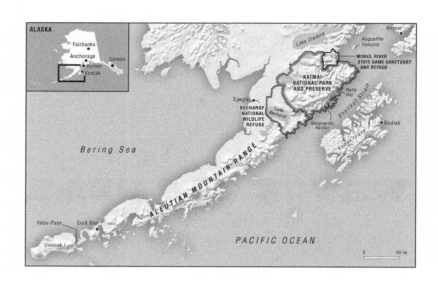

**Map 1.** Lake Becharof, McNeil River, and the Alaska Peninsula.
Created by Erin Greb.

# Introduction

Their [human and bear] history together has been rich and primal. The bear has represented fearful evil and, at other times, regenerative power. The bear is not only complex, but ambiguous and contradictory.

—Paul Shepard and Barry Sanders, *The Sacred Paw*

Late September. I'm alone and sitting on a tundra-covered hillside at the eastern end of Lake Becharof, Alaska, watching Slade, a huge, fully grown brown bear, who could weigh close to a thousand pounds. He's walking along a bear trail that connects two creeks, each full of dead, dying, and spawned-out red salmon. His new winter coat catches the light from the low-angle fall sun, which gives his dark brown hair silvery highlights. If he continues, he'll pass about a hundred feet from me.

Queen Elizabeth and her two yearling cubs are eating blueberries near the trail Slade is using. I've been watching for several hours, taking notes on their activities. I've been hoping for another bear to come along the well-used path so I can see some sort of interaction, envisioning that one of the area's legion of "subadult" bears might wander by and Queen Elizabeth, being a protective mother, would charge and chase.

Instead I get Slade, a real treat, and a bear I don't see every day. When Slade is still a few hundred yards from the bear family, they stop eating and slowly amble off. They give no indication, other than their timely departure, that they sense his approach. Likewise, Slade shows no sign he knows they are there, continuing his characteristic, head-down, pigeon-toed walk.

A steady wind blows from Slade's direction toward the mother and

1

cubs. I can guess, but certainly not prove, that Queen Elizabeth caught his scent, recognized it as coming from a male, and moved away, wishing to avoid physical confrontation and possible predation to her cubs.

When Slade nears me, he stops and lifts his head. His face gives no hint of tension, his ears remain up, and his mouth stays closed. His eyes seem to lock on mine and we give each other a long, hard stare.

Abruptly he drops his bottom jaw, his large lower canines flash, and for a brief moment he raises his right nostril and tosses his head before quickly turning away and disappearing down the bear trail toward the creek.

I remain sitting, doing my best to write down objective notes of our interaction—distance, time, weather, wind direction, and behavior—but while I am writing I am also thinking: Did Slade just sneer at me?

• • •

In 1966, when I was twenty-one, I began to watch and follow brown bears. I've continued to do this for more than fifty years.

*Watch the Bear* is memoir, anecdote, and science. It's my story of how I have come to understand bears. It's based on my research and observations and mine alone.

When I began I had no idea how to go about being with bears. I'd never even seen a brown bear. I didn't know what they would allow or what I should do. However, I soon realized that being in the presence of bears required a certain level of responsiveness on my part and a willingness to abide by rules the bears so clearly showed me.

Somewhere along the way I put away my misconceptions about aggression and started treating bears as bears. The more I watched them, the more I understood the fear people had was an overreaction. It was almost as though humans perceived bears not as bears, but as dangerous people.

Year after year I went into the field. I watched and followed. I quietly sat while Slade and Queen Elizabeth and hundreds of others walked by and did extraordinary things. Sometimes I was part of the landscape, other times the focus of their attention.

• • •

In 2000, after years of conducting research as both an undergraduate and graduate student, working for the Alaska Department of Fish and Game, and watching bears by myself, I decided to make my avocation my vocation and started a business guiding photographers, filmmakers, and interested people into the wild specifically to see bears. I still do this today.

In coastal Alaska, where I offer my bear trips, this creature goes by the scientifically correct name *Ursus arctos*, a brown bear. In the interior of the state, away from the sea, this same bear is referred to as a grizzly.

Some of my clients, particularly men suffering from what I call "tooth and claw syndrome," want to see grizzlies, not brown bears. Evidently, it makes a person very brave to have been near an animal with a fearsome reputation, sharp teeth and claws, and the terrifying but now unused Latin name *Ursus horribilis*. Maybe they imagine returning home with hero shots of themselves sitting next to this scary creature.

· · ·

Whether we consider them trophy or nuisance, delight, monster, mythical creature, spiritual being, or the link between ourselves and nature, we are far from the first to contemplate our relationship with bears. My family yells at the winter moose on the path to our house as they impede our progress and block the way to the school bus. Yet we remain quiet when coyotes howl, hoping they will come closer. We make meals difficult for passing black bears by never leaving food outside. Yet we hope a brown bear will feel welcome and come through our garden for a feast of broccoli.

After a lifetime of rural living, we have learned to constantly modify our behavior toward the animals living nearby in an attempt to live as peacefully with them as we can, believing we are building a life that can accommodate all species—especially bears.

· · ·

I've presented bears through this writer's eyes. It is my hope that you, the reader, if new to bears, will have their world opened to you. Or if you're a seasoned visitor to bear country, you may see things through the eyes of another that will intrigue and challenge you. And I hope that you will feel respect and commitment to the bear's right to a place in the world of man.

So, what of Slade? He disappears into the alders that border the creek. I hear him splash as he chases unseen fish. Thirty minutes later he appears on the far bank following a bear trail that I know continues on for several miles to the top of the creek. He stays in sight for several minutes before sauntering around a bend and out of sight. Queen Elizabeth and her two? They move several hundred yards and resume their berry picking on an open hillside. One cub manages to flush a ptarmigan family, doubtlessly intent on picking the same berries.

And me? With no bears close by I lie back for a short nap before beginning the evening walk back to camp.

# ONE

## BEGINNINGS

# 1

## We Thought the World Would Never Run Out of Wild Animals

**M**y mother kept diaries and photo journals of every hunting trip she ever went on. Before I could read, I spent hours looking at the pictures. In a photograph of my mother, grandfather, and three uncles taken in Kenya in the 1920s, each of them holds up the head of a black-maned African lion—that morning's bag.

I come from a family of hunters.

The living room floor of our home was covered with the skins of these same lions, mounted with open-mouthed snarls. Along with the lions were rugs made from brown bears shot in Alaska, British Columbia, and the Yukon. For years I slept under a Dall sheep head, killed by my mother in Alaska not far from where I live today.

Remnants of what my relatives killed and used for killing endured. Beautiful handcrafted double-barreled rifles made in England—elephant guns. Dozens of mounted animal heads—Cape buffalo and antelope from Africa and moose, sheep, goats, and caribou from North America. Wastepaper baskets made from the feet and lower legs of rhinos and elephants. A full-size ostrich mount. Skins of leopards, cheetahs, and zebras—the zebra heads were elsewhere, if indeed they had ever been mounted. Would you put a horse's head on your wall? One uncle had three tiger skins in his house, from tigers killed in what was then known as Indochina, today's Vietnam.

My mother hunted tigers, too. She sat for days in a blind next to a tethered goat, which was meant to attract a tiger. I imagine her alone in the jungle, twenty years old, with long blond hair, jodhpurs, and the knee-high leather boots I would later play in, clutching a rifle custom-made just for her. She was a well-known beauty with marriage proposals beyond number, an All-American field hockey player, and the apple of her father's eye. When the tiger finally appeared, she missed.

As I sat on her lap, she didn't tell me nursery rhymes; she told me of safaris and pack trips. She described how my grandfather always wanted to visit the Peace River of Alberta and British Columbia—the "Mighty Peace," as she liked to say. He never made it.

She told me about eating elephant and enjoying a dinner of "Tommy"—Thomson's gazelle. I can't recall her ever saying she ate bear. I do know she once killed an Alaskan brown bear at dusk and arrived back at camp many hours later to her worried father playing solitaire by lantern light.

Her tales all had a common thread—they were about the country, the landscape, and her father, not about the shot or the trophy. When pressed about dead rhinos and elephants, she'd express remorse and often add, "Times were different then. We thought the world would never run out of wild animals."

My head was full of images of her adventures. Crossing the Atlantic in a steamer, admiring the apes on Gibraltar, sailing the Mediterranean to Egypt where she, her brothers, and father rode camels in front of the pyramids. Then the journey down the Suez and into the Indian Ocean, on to Mombasa and Nairobi and the hunting lands to the east. The Serengeti occupied far more of my childhood thoughts than heaven or football.

I never questioned killing for fun. I just wanted to do it, to be like my uncles, mother, and grandfather.

• • •

My successful and hardworking parents expected the same of their children. I can't remember ever taking naps. We always had "jobs" and were expected to help. At meals, they asked us to contribute to the conversation, whether it was about famous men and women, books, ideas, music, art, or politics.

As well as operating a profitable dairy farm, my father's vocation and passion were architecture and sculpture. His legacy includes stadiums, apartment buildings, houses, and beautiful fountains made with bronze figures. Books he authored are still in print and portraits he created of renowned people attest to his talents.

A city person, he knew little of animals. The few times we hunted together, he proved to be a very poor shot. Not shooting straight might have been his only failure and I doubt if he admitted it to himself. He was egotistical, creative, fiercely competitive, and not prone to listening.

By the time I came along, my grandfather had died and my uncles had turned into ardent conservationists who no longer hunted. My mother had given up her rifle for academia—attending the Bank Street College of Education and becoming a well-known expert in early childhood education. A cooperative nursery school she created still exists almost ninety years later. Learning through play is the foundation for the educational philosophy of that school, and I am certain it was the conversations with her that gave me my life-long interest in the play behavior of bears.

She put up with all manner of dead fur-bearing animals, ducks, and pheasants I left hanging on the back porch. My three sisters refused to walk past the carnage and never used the back door during the fall and winter. Iron-willed yet self-effacing, my mother let my father rage and pontificate.

My father's greatest influence on me also took place before I was born. Oskar Stonorov grew up in Germany and his two best friends lived nearby. One friend's father, a noted physician, took all three boys under his wing. He must have stressed the arts and sciences, as my father ended up an internationally known sculptor and architect. Another boy, Erik Erikson, became one of the foremost psychoanalysts of the twentieth century. We considered him and his brilliant wife, Joan, the god and goddess of our family. Equally important was the third boy, Peter Blos, and his wife, Merta. Like Erik, Peter was a pioneering psychoanalyst. The friendship formed in those years lasted throughout their lives, and during frequent visits Peter and Erik kept the lid on Oskar, something not many could do.

I discovered what would become my field, ethology—the biology of animal behavior—on my own, but after my father's death Peter and Erik encouraged me in this subject, one that ever since has consumed me. While at Harvard, Erik introduced me to Irven DeVore, a leader in the field of behavioral primatology. And Peter knew Konrad Lorenz, one of the founding fathers of ethology—I kick myself for not going to Germany to meet Lorenz. Peter was also an expert on adolescence, something I had recently experienced. His book *On Adolescence* is still used today as a basic teaching text.

Both Peter and Erik had this magical, calm way of talking, explaining, and listening. I pride myself, likely without foundation, that my diminutive ability to ask the right research question comes from listening and reading the books of these two people. My father approved of the study of behavior—after all, Erik and Peter were his friends and peers—but he also believed success meant moving to the top of one's profession.

It would be years before I would hear about the fields of cognitive neuroscience, behavioral ecology, or sociobiology—but I could read a book by Erik or Peter and wonder if what I was reading about humans might be applicable to the study of animals. I began to imagine how an animal's behavior might continue to develop and change as it grew and matured. Later, when I had actually begun to watch bears, I started to think of them exhibiting different behaviors as they moved through readily apparent life stages.

I had already watched the lives of countless animals during my childhood. Our Pennsylvania farm grew food and provided pasture for eighty dairy cows plus pigs, chickens, and horses. Along with 150 acres of cultivated fields, there were hundreds of acres of woods and swamp that protected and propagated wildlife. Almost two miles of a healthy and clear flowing stream meant swimming and endless hours of fishing.

From the earliest years I spent most of my time outdoors, working on the farm during summers, weekends, and after school. When not milking or caring for animals, I spent the majority of my time making hay, an activity that started in the spring and continued into fall. Six decades later I can walk those fields and still locate half-hidden rocks too large to blow up or bulldoze, laying partially exposed and ready to break the cutter bar on a hay mower.

We always had at least four dogs, one for each child in the family. They were usually present for meals, lying under the kitchen table. Every few weeks a raucous fight would break out over a food scrap, doubtlessly dropped by me and not by my neat and tidy sisters. Not surprisingly, the most favored dog spot was beneath my chair. The table stretched along a stone wall making things underneath a bit dark—a regular dog den.

Perhaps fights weren't only about food but for floor position. When they happened I'd just pick up my feet and the dogs would quickly work things out—only occasionally would there be blood. The whole family knew there was a top dog.

Today I'd say four dogs being fed under a table quickly develop a recognizable hierarchy maintained by periodic dominance displays. And these dogs were farm dogs—they were never tied up, they came and went as they pleased, and they acted as a pack. Many a ground hog caught away from its borrow succumbed to their hunts.

When I was eight I was given a horse of my own, a mare named Good Cheer. She and I ranged far and wide through the rural township. She was faithful and calm as I lived out my Wild West explorer fantasies in this pastoral Pennsylvania landscape.

I was also fast friends with Rosie and Mabel, the last two giant Percherons from my grandfather's prizewinning herd. Old and wise enough to no longer need fences, they were allowed to wander wherever they wanted. To this day my sisters and I remember Mabel's habit of poking her huge head into the kitchen. I have a picture of Rosie receiving a trophy at a horse show with the caption "Rosie, two years old—2,000 pounds."

Then there was Old Dan. He had a brand on his flank—almost unheard of in our locale, a land of thoroughbred hunters and jumpers—and we were told he once herded cows in the Chicago stockyards. This might have been true as he could turn on a dime. Retired and put out to pasture, he'd tolerate as many children as could fit on his broad back, stopping, turning, and then nuzzling any that slid off.

I never doubted horses knew what I was feeling. It wasn't something to be learned and analyzed, it just was.

Growing up, I killed many different things. I didn't shoot songbirds, opossums, or skunks because, to quote my mother, they were "nice to have around." I did slaughter—in great numbers, I'm sorry to say—English sparrows, starlings, and pigeons. My mother granted permission: "It's ok to shoot them—they were introduced."

I also targeted crows, frogs, snakes, groundhogs, and the occasional fox. I caught muskrats and raccoons in traps. Of course I hunted rabbits, squirrels, pheasants, woodcock, grouse, ducks, and deer. I started out with spears, slingshots, bows and arrows, and moved on to BB guns and air rifles when I was six. Next came small-caliber rifles, then shotguns, and finally around puberty I graduated to bigger guns and hunting with what Pennsylvanians call "deer rifles." I was a model rural kid, seldom seen without a weapon of some kind.

My chief hunting companion was Kyle. He lived on a farm about two miles from ours. A relocated Texan, he was raised to think anything that moved was his for the taking. He regularly shot hawks, which rode the thermals above the ridge behind his house. Before that, he was renowned for killing barn swallows with his slingshot.

The hawk hunting spot had been used by area farmers for generations. Hundreds of spent shotgun shells littered the ground. Locals knew the best times for shooting were spring and fall when the hawks migrated.

One afternoon, Kyle's grandfather, a very hard and gruff man, stormed into their kitchen from next door and berated Kyle for bringing home a pheasant that looked like it had been "ground-sluiced." That means shot while on the ground.

I knew it had been an overhead shot, made at extremely close range. In that family, shooting game on the ground was as bad as walking naked into church—it just wasn't done. However, killing a sharp-shinned or red-tailed hawk for target practice was okay. My family didn't kill hawks; we just watched them. But when I was ten, I got a new rifle for my birthday, and my mother and I spent the day driving around the countryside so I could shoot crows out of the car window.

The two farms Kyle and I hunted spanned more than seven hundred acres. We knew every cover, every trail, and which direction a game bird would likely flush.

You have to know where the animals are to be a successful hunter. You learn the seasons through your prey. You learn what animals eat at different times of the year. You know when, where, and for how long they rest.

When I started to watch bears in 1966, I did nothing more than take what I learned on the farm and apply it. Fencerows turned into salmon streams, wood lots to alder patches, swamps to tidal estuaries. I'd amaze clients when we visited Hallo Bay in Katmai National Park—back in the days when there were still lots of bears and razor clams. I'd pick a spot in the tidal flats, sit down, and almost always have a clamming brown bear feed up to where we were sitting.

My "magic" consisted of knowing the clams were more plentiful and easiest to dig in what I called sand lenses, raised ridges of fine sand and gravel that occurred in certain spots. I'd look for a bear digging at the end of one of these places and go sit down at the other. If we sat quietly, the bear would feed right up to and eventually around us.

Once on a photo shoot for *Men's Vogue*, I did this with a mother and two yearling cubs. They fed in our direction as the New York photographer snapped away. Closer and closer, the bears kept digging—a mature bear can dig more than sixty clams an hour given enough clams. The bears dug and ate while the photographer shot, that is until I became worried they would try to dig directly underneath where he was crouching. I stood up when the female bear was about five feet away. She and her cubs moved off a few feet and went right on digging and eating. The photographer got some good images.

• • •

In 1970 my father was killed in a plane crash. He was doing what he wanted: working to make the world a better place, combining education, public service, labor unions, and good architecture.

At the very end of his life, as part of a larger project for the United Automobile Workers and his great friend and union president Walter Reuther, my father created individual bronze sculptures of the twelve signs of the Zodiac as they had appeared on Walter's birthday. The figures were placed inside a round meditation room at the Walter and May Reuther UAW Family Education Center in Michigan.

The crash, which also killed Walter and May, occurred shortly after he finished the project but before I could question him as to what his intentions and beliefs were.

So, why did he include the alignment of the stars? Well, why not? After all, Harvey Fisher, who had the farm next to ours, planted by the moon. Everything always came up and he almost lived to a hundred.

I have learned that bears move according to the tide, the light, and the seasons. Certainly, they are influenced by the four elements of astrology: fire, earth, air, and water. Alaska brown bears are born in dens during January or February. This makes them either Capricorns or Aquarians.

I like to think my father and mother believed as I do that there is no end to what influences us—emotionally, spiritually, or physically.

# 2

## Causation and Function

Niko Tinbergen's greatest contribution to biology was probably the simple logic that he applied to disentangle our questions about behavior.

—Hans Kruuk, *Niko's Nature*

igh school was awful. I spent most of my time reading books that weren't assigned in class, hunting, partying, building car engines, and hiding my learning disabilities. Many academic subjects made no sense.

However, I managed to graduate and after a couple of years of moving around Pennsylvania, Arizona, and Alaska, I enrolled at Goddard College in Vermont. My academic life changed. I discovered through independent study that I could learn in my own way and it was permissible to skip things I couldn't understand. I didn't need chemistry or calculus to read Jack Kerouac.

Today's Goddard College website says the place is "a one of a kind institution of higher education with a history of creativity and chaos, invention and experimentation, of growth, decline and reemergence." This was certainly true in 1964, when I arrived, and pretty much sums up my three-year learning experience there.

I heard Allen Ginsberg and Peter Orlovsky read poetry. Stokely Carmichael visited, and Archie Shepp sometimes played jazz in the student union. Students took turns driving an ancient Ford to New York City to make certain we always had a good supply of dope to smoke.

I arrived curious about the science of animal behavior. I'd discovered the topic on my own as I read science books almost constantly, even in those wandering years after high school. When I realized I could study something that interested me, I knew I wanted to make this subject the focus of my education. Goddard required a thesis to graduate and, in a life-determining moment of genius, I picked the behavior of bears to investigate and write about.

And so I began my career in ethology, or animal behavior. While the term ethology isn't used much today, I still occasionally employ it when asked what my field is.

It was a burgeoning subject—a lot of what we consider the classics today did not yet exist. While I was in Vermont I read the papers of Peter Marler and Robert Hinde, but they would not publish their definitive texts until 1966. Jane Goodall was still at Gombe with her chimps, working on her PhD—*In the Shadow of Man* didn't appear until 1971. Dian Fossey wouldn't begin her gorilla study until 1966. George Schaller, a well-known wildlife biologist who quickly became one of my academic heroes, published *The Mountain Gorilla* in 1963 and *The Deer and the Tiger* in 1967. Andy Russell's wonderful book *Grizzly Country*, which came out in 1967, had a profound influence on my observation techniques and initial interpretations of bear behavior.

Then after a single reading, the Dutch scientist Niko Tinbergen's 1951 book, *The Study of Instinct*, and his 1963 paper, "On Aims and Methods of Ethology," became my bibles.

In the paper he discusses his famous "Four Whys"—causation, development, function, and evolution. I use these to this day.

Here's what happens. We ask a question about a certain behavior: Why does an animal behave the way it does? Why does the cock crow at sunrise? Or, why would a female bear with cubs avoid mature males?

Then we look at the Four Whys. The first question to be considered would be causation. What causes the avoidance? What causes her to move away from him? What triggers the behavior? What is happening before she moves with her cubs?

Tinbergen's second question would consider development or ontogeny of behavior. Why and how did the bear develop this behavior? How is avoidance behavior affected by learning and environmental influences? Did this behavior come about during the lifetime of the female bear? Is it in fact learned behavior?

The third question is about function. What is the function of the avoidance behavior? Why is she doing that? What is the survival value of this behavior?

And the last question would look at evolution. How and why did this behavior come about as the species of brown bear evolved? Here we may get into anything from taxonomy and comparisons between species to Charles Darwin. I learned to do my research using all four questions and never to question one without taking into account the others.

Along with thousands of other people, I read Conrad Lorenz's popular 1963 book, *On Aggression*. The human implications for his theories on aggression were somewhat interesting, but I found his animal research and observations far more so and aligned to my way of thinking. Tinbergen and Lorenz, along with Karl von Frisch, won the Nobel Prize for their ethological contributions in 1973.

I'm not sure how education works—what one keeps and discards—but I haven't strayed far from Tinbergen's ideas or his mantra. They've served me well and I share them with my clients—we gain little by speculating on the subjective experience of animals, and we can't really know about their emotions.

I can't count all of the times I've heard people say, "The bear was really mad!" when describing their adverse interaction. Much as I like conjecture—it can make for a fun game—I always try to avoid defining a bear's mental or emotional state when I see one exhibiting a particular behavior.

I spent most of my time at Goddard reading. There weren't any brown bears around and no single teacher who could walk me through the kind of research project I was envisioning. It was the Goddard way—learning through independent study. It worked for me.

# 3

## Meeting Molly

One day, early in the fall of 1964, I saw a beautiful blonde walking across the Goddard cafeteria. She sat down, I went over and must have said the right thing. I've shared my life with Molly since that day. Five-foot-two with eyes of blue, she was barely eighteen years old.

She'd never camped out, confronted a bear, cooked on a fire, bathed in an ice-cold lake, or been out of touch with the outside world. A product of a private girl's school, she was well educated and far smarter than me.

In our first five years together, she never missed a bear trip. In the days before electric fences were used to keep bears out of tents and bear-proof containers to keep them out of food, she became adept at beating pan lids together to scare them away from camp. She took hundreds of pages of notes and filled in innumerable data sheets. She cooked, spent days wet and cold, kept our spirits up, and never complained or chastised me for my many mistakes.

She didn't know what she was getting into when she arrived in Egegik, Alaska, that first summer. She'd gone to a boutique in Philadelphia to get outfitted and purchased a pair of stylish leather hiking boots with stacked heels. The boots were fine for Chestnut Street but were no match for the rugged and wet Alaska Peninsula. A heel came off on the first day. I took her to the Egegik store and set her up with rubber "cannery" boots.

When we returned from the field at the end of each season with the bears, she supported me and helped me organize my thoughts and data. I have no doubt she got me through both undergraduate and graduate school.

Molly had also grown up on a farm and knew about chickens, turkeys, sheep, and pigs, and how important a small place can be. She had a horse named Brownie and was never without dogs and cats, but while I was out hunting with Kyle, she was quietly watching animals and writing poems with her grandmother. In college she studied early childhood education and to this day knows more about both human and animal behavior than I do. A licensed clinical therapist, she left me behind long ago in her academic accomplishments.

We have more than fifty years of stories together as a couple, as parents, and as grandparents. She remembers the times I'd smoke cigarettes in a skiff loaded down with four 55-gallon drums of gas, and the night we spent in a leaky tent with two wet sleeping bags and only a very thin, foil-faced "space" blanket between us and subfreezing temperatures.

I remember the early years when she could identify individual bears just as well as I did, but still laugh about the dark and stormy night we inadvertently pitched our tent in the middle of a well-worn bear trail—and the time she watched a bear try to get its tongue into an empty beer bottle left outside.

Thanks to Molly, I've discovered that women understand animals far better than men do. Men tend to see wild creatures as hard-wired and similar to each other. Women, on the other hand, understand more, and see animals as individuals—each different and each important.

Another woman who had an impact on my work was Sykes Equine. Sykes was in her midthirties and taking classes at Goddard. Red-haired, tall, and willowy, she always had men nearby. Maybe she wasn't Jane Goodall, but she was certainly her intellectual equal. Although life dealt her a few blows and she never had the opportunity to study chimps with Richard Leaky, she nevertheless was a keen observer and interpreter of the behavior of animals and was unlike anyone I have ever met.

While it was the '60s in Vermont with lots of drugs, wine drinking, and conversation going on, Sykes often sat quietly in her own private world. Perhaps because she had been a professional mime for many years she was used to being silent, only looking outward—watching and observing.

Molly would often entertain Sykes's young daughter, Rain, by reading animal stories. Rain's father, Michael Equine, was the drummer for the rock band Cat Mother and the All-Night Newsboys, and wasn't around. Sykes jokingly said she married him because of his last name. Like Molly and me, she loved horses and had spent much of her youth riding through the Mississippi Delta.

She and Rain lived in a menagerie. At one time she had a dog named Useless—a few years later we named a bear after him. There was a German shepherd, tomcats named Beaslie and Tuffy, and Zachery, a domestic rabbit. Coming and going when they felt like it was a porcupine named Jimmy Familiar and a skunk named Sweet William.

One night Sykes came home to find Jimmy had opened the door and was eating out of the cat's bowl while the cats perched on top of the bookcase watching him. Sweet William never learned to open the door but would wait on the porch until someone let him in.

She liked to interpret the personalities and behavior of her pets, and I learned from her. At her house, skunks weren't skunks spraying the unwary, but rather the "marvelous" Sweet William. She referred to him as timid and shy, and said that he loved blueberries.

As part of a Goddard class, Sykes, Molly, and I wrote an essay about the comparatively new science of ethology and presented it at a New England college symposium. Sykes presented the paper to students from Ivy League colleges who were no doubt receiving educations that were the antithesis of what was going on at Goddard. Regardless, it was well received, and we were swamped with questions about Tinbergen and Lorenz.

Juan was the sometime lover of Sykes. I knew him as a connecting point between the outside natural world and the inner world of Sykes's living room. He was a great jazz pianist and he had played with some of the best bands in New York. His mother was a New Yorker, his father a country person from the Philippines. He soaked up so many stories from his father that he understood how things worked in the jungle and forest. Juan seemed to glide when he walked—it was not an affectation, it was simply the way he moved—with grace and complete silence.

Juan carried a special gun called a drilling. He and I were probably the only people in that part of Vermont who knew what a drilling was—an expensive handmade weapon used in Europe that never seemed to catch on in the United States. "Drilling" is German for triplet, and the guns have three barrels—two shotgun barrels on top for shooting birds and a rifle barrel underneath for killing animals.

Juan would wander the hills of Vermont with this beautiful firearm. But he never killed anything, and I don't think he ever intended to. When you walked with him, you became part of the outdoors, slipping through and between things. You became the Indian of your childhood moving silently through the trees.

Juan spent hours in the woods watching animals, and I went with him as much as I could. Mostly we'd go out, spot a few deer, and just sit and see what the deer did. Sometimes we'd watch a groundhog, or if we were lucky a ruffed grouse. Juan would sit quietly, his only motion an occasional shy smile.

He taught me there was no need to continually explain to enter an animal's world—just be happy the animal wants to share with you. What I took from him was to remember that what you are seeing is only a point in time, an experience to be savored for the moment.

I learned new things about observing wildlife from Juan—how to let the animals pick the distance they were comfortable with, how to tell if they were at ease, and how to simply let things happen.

All this stimulus and exposure to new ideas added up to me actually paying attention in school. Imagine it: I've got this intellectual girlfriend, this eccentric skunk-whisperer friend, and this smooth-walking, jazz-playing son of the jungle as mentors. Fellow college students are rioting about race and war; they're building subdivisions where I used to hunt; and my high school friends are getting killed in Vietnam. My little sister is marching in Birmingham; Stokely Carmichael is yelling "Black Power"; Allen Ginsberg is writing poems about making love to his partner, Peter; and the car I built, a customized 500-horsepower Jaguar xk140 capable of speeds in excess of 150 miles an hour, is ready to go.

I was an idealistic twenty-year-old and not about to write a thesis or spend a moment of my time on something that didn't push the limits of knowledge and improve the human condition.

I knew I needed to go back to Alaska and see some bears.

# 4

## My Best Choice

*Just what a wise old grizzly would say while philosophizing concerning the white race would be of human interest and rich in material for literature.*

—Enos A. Mills, *The Grizzly: Our Greatest Wild Animal*

In April of 1966, I pulled out of Plainfield, Vermont—in the Jaguar—and drove to Alaska. Alone, I made the 4,500-mile trip in five long days.

Once there, Howard "Howie" Bass—a person I'd met in previous summers while working as a carpenter in Fairbanks—and I cobbled together a plan to spend the summer filming and observing brown bears. Molly stayed in school and the plan was for her to join me in late July.

A great intellect who was prone to long silences, Howie, like Sykes Equine, often withdrew from other people, endlessly writing scripts and planning shots for future films. We were ideal traveling companions, as I also liked not talking all the time.

He was a talented visual artist and writer. Somewhere I saw a self-portrait in clay he'd made—it was an exact likeness. At least six foot two and immensely powerful, he was capable of carrying a heavy pack and his Arriflex movie camera, mounted on a wooden tripod, hour after hour and day after day. In addition to an MFA from the University of Alaska, he held another degree from the prestigious UCLA Film School, as well as a BA from Williams College, where he had been a winning giant slalom ski racer. Howie had family money and the finances to do whatever he wanted, so we had the best camera equipment money could buy. Howie also had no fear of bears, was seemingly impervious to being cold and wet, and never seemed to tire.

Molly and I remember returning to camp one evening and watching Howie standing in the stern of our skiff wearing his ever-present leather shirt, soaked in the freezing rain. He never shivered or complained, but his lips were completely blue.

Our trip plans were simple: Howie wanted to make a film about bears; I wanted to study them. I'd worked on a couple of forest fires for the U.S. Forest Service in Fairbanks in the late spring—something you could always do in those days—and saved enough money for my share of the proposed trip.

Now the only question was where to go. After much research, we picked Lake Becharof, on the Alaska Peninsula. Our decision was thanks to the advice of Phil Kelly, a University of Alaska student we knew who'd grown up in the nearby Bristol Bay village of Egegik. He'd been going up the Egegik River to Lake Becharof since he was a boy and assured us we'd have little company there as we photographed and watched bears.

The little company part was very important. I'd considered the McNeil River State Game Sanctuary on Lower Cook Inlet—I'd later spend a total of twelve summers there—but I also learned the Alaska Department of Fish and Game would be there capturing and marking bears as part of a research project. The last thing we wanted to watch was a bear being shot with tranquilizing darts and being chased by state employees. Going instead to Becharof remains one of the best choices I have ever made.

Before we left for Becharof, I read everything I could about bears in Alaska. Much has been written over the years—mostly, but not always, about killing bears. These are some of volumes I read that spring and ones I keep on my shelf today: *The Wild Grizzlies of Alaska*, written in 1930 by John M. Holzworth and one of the first books to mention the conservation of bears in our state; and *The Minds and Manners of Wild Animals*, which is a plea for more study and less killing, written in 1922 by W. T. Hornaday, then head of the New York Zoological Park. My favorite quotes from that book include "The most interesting thing about a wild animal is its mind and its reasoning" and "A dead animal is only a poor decaying thing." Other titles include the still timely classic *No Room for Bears*, written in 1965 by Frank Dufresne, among the first to call for brown bear conservation in Southeast Alaska; and *The Grizzly*, by Enos A. Mills, which remains, in spite of being published in 1919, the classic brown bear book. Mills took more information to the grave than I possess after fifty years with bears—and he wasn't bogged down by Tinbergen's Four Whys every time he tried to understand something he was seeing.

Most importantly, I read everything I could find that came out of John and Frank Craighead's ongoing Yellowstone studies of brown bears. I paid special attention to the pioneering behavioral information of Robert L. Ruff and Maurice Hornocker, both of whom worked on the Craighead projects.

I was ready.

In May of 1966 Howie and I flew from Anchorage to King Salmon, where we crammed our gear into the twin-engine mail plane to make the forty-mile flight down the coast to Egegik.

Neither of us had ever seen a brown bear.

# 5

## Egegik and Akutaq

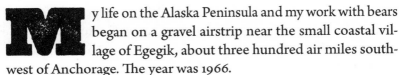y life on the Alaska Peninsula and my work with bears began on a gravel airstrip near the small coastal village of Egegik, about three hundred air miles southwest of Anchorage. The year was 1966.

My first memory is Howie and I standing next to a huge pile of camping gear, watching the plane that brought us disappear into the distance. I was twenty-two years old, a model hippie with long hair and a beard.

Half a mile down a slight hill I could see the houses of the village and the weathered gray buildings of the salmon canneries; beyond a wide river, the far shore barely visible. The village sat stark and abrupt in the landscape, no slow beginnings or strung-out endings—just suddenly there in a sea of grasses, willow, and alder.

A few children came running from the direction of town. They giggled and kept asking why we were there until an old pickup arrived and many little hands helped stow our belongings. We climbed with all the kids onto the tailgate and made our way into town. There we met the mother of our friend from Fairbanks. At her house four women were talking in English and what I guessed to be Yupik. They served us coffee and smiled at us as my friend's mother politely asked questions about why we had come to Egegik. When we answered, "to watch and film bears," both the Yupik and smiles increased.

We finished our coffee and someone's child showed us the way down to the town beach on the Egegik River. Even today a few people in Egegik remember the hippies who came to watch bears on Lake Becharof.

When the weather was fair the beach became our place in the village. In those days if you stood on the south shore of the east-west running river and faced north toward Naknek and King Salmon, some forty miles away, you'd see the factory complex and wharf of the Alaska Packers Cannery on your right. To the left a few hundred yards away was Egegik Packers, smaller, but with another high wharf able to accommodate twenty-five-foot-high tides, which occurred every month.

Howie and I watched as both canneries prepared for the commercial salmon season just a few weeks away. Fishing boats were being pulled by tractors from huge storage sheds and placed in the water by steam-powered cranes. Left in the sheds, except for a few that had been converted to power, were the famous Bristol Bay "double enders," sailboats that were once used to net salmon.

We walked a half mile or so up river, past the last sign of humans, and made ourselves a camp just above the tide line. Aside from sleeping and cooking, I spent the next few weeks back at the town beach— talking, drinking, and watching the boats—enjoying the pestering of the village kids, hearing stories, and feeling badly because I had none that could equal those being told.

I asked lots of questions of everyone who stopped by to talk, questions about the country and the bears up the river and on Lake Becharof. We seldom lacked someone to talk to.

Neither of us had ever experienced village life and the friendliness and hospitality that are part of it. We loved the people and the pace and were in no hurry to go. Why leave a place when you are having fun?

Upon hearing of our plans, village residents suggested we wait ten days for the big tides of the month before heading up river. The Egegik River is tidal for most of its length and shallow in spots. We were told high water would make travel far easier. To this day I am a firm believer in local knowledge, whether it be about bears, tides, terrain, or weather.

In those days plywood "setnet" skiffs for the salmon industry were built in Egegik. Twenty to twenty-five feet in length, these small boats were especially made to remove fish from "set" gillnets, nets that have one end tied or "set" on shore and the other end anchored out in the current to intercept migrating salmon as they swim upstream. The skiffs were made with four-to-six-inch-wide solid wood gunnels, rounded at the edges, so nets full of salmon could be easily pulled aboard.

Powered by fifty-horsepower outboard engines, the boats were fast and were the equivalent of hot rods in Egegik. One way to be a really cool village kid was to approach the beach in your skiff at full power—maybe twenty-five or thirty miles an hour—while standing in the stern and holding onto the engine tiller and throttle. At the magic moment you turn off the engine, then tilt it—put it in the up position—to lock the propeller out of the water. Next you leap onto the gunnel, run from the stern to bow, and jump off, as the boat slows to a stop in the soft sand of the beach. All the while looking calm and relaxed.

Try it sometime. Possible broken limbs await should you fall into the boat, a soaking and humiliation if you go over the side. We quickly dubbed this feat an "Egegik Landing"—and women, children, and old people didn't do it. I tried a few times, but always very slowly.

In the mid-1960s the red or sockeye salmon runs in Bristol Bay—the world's largest wild salmon fishery—were small. Some years saw catches of fewer than five million fish, compared to a twenty-five million average between 1980 and 2012. Due to better fishery management, a few recent years have seen runs of almost fifty million salmon.

With a small harvest predicted for 1966, people in Egegik weren't looking toward the upcoming season with any great hopes. The arrival of Howie and me in this lean year must have been a bit of an oddity. We hadn't come to catch or buy fish. We weren't trying to make money. We'd come to learn about bears.

Although snowy, out-of-focus television had entered village homes, residents were still great storytellers. As I listened, Lake Becharof started to take shape in my mind.

I met two men who claimed to have shot and killed twenty-six bears in one day when they were teenagers on Lake Becharof. Slightly remorseful now, some years later, they still gave the impression the bears had no particular value; and because bears sometimes came near the village and got into fishing nets and even broke into cabins, they were in fact a nuisance.

This was contrary to what I was expecting to hear—my belief, based on my reading, was that brown bears held a special and sacred place in the Aleut culture.

I met another man whose father had been severely mauled by a brown bear while moose hunting. In the years since the incident, his father had killed every bear he'd seen. Oddly, the son said he actually liked bears, sometimes hiding when they approached, letting them come to within fifteen or twenty feet before jumping up and yelling at them. He said he was always amazed at how frightened the bears appeared before bounding away.

An old man named Deacon, who spoke only Yupik, and his wife were far different people. They were living in a white wall tent on the town beach. She cared for him as he had lost most of his fingers due to frostbite. Like us, they were planning to leave in a month or so to go up to the head of the Egegik River to spend the summer living their subsistence lifestyle. With one exception, they had been the last people to spend winters in a cabin on Lake Becharof, something many families had done in the past.

From what I understood as his wife translated in hesitant English, Deacon had very little to say about bears. He shared no heroic bear stories or advice and I got the feeling the bears simply lived around the lake and so did he. Deacon was a fox trapper. He netted fish in the lake in the fall, froze them if the weather permitted, and when bears denned and the eagles had left, he put the fish out on the hillside behind his house. Foxes came from far and wide and when their fur looked to be at its glossy full prime, Deacon would set out his traps.

Another summer we met Deacon and his wife at the top of the Egegik River. Their ancient outboard motor had quit and Deacon's frostbitten hands couldn't make a repair. After a few hours of cleaning the carburetor, I got the engine running.

As I worked, Molly hung out with the elderly couple in their tattered wall tent where she was offered porcupine and the local version of *akutaq*. This Inuit and Aleut food is usually comprised of wild animal fat, sugar, and berries—but in this case it was a mixture of sugar, powdered milk, blueberries, and Crisco. It was the first and last time Molly dined on porcupine.

People told us of another lake resident who was in Anchorage that summer. No one knew when "Crazy Billy" Nekeferoff would return. Rumor had it he disliked any visitors to Lake Becharof and some of his trapping partners had disappeared over the years. He'd been accused of murder more than once and at one point served some time. In later years we discovered crudely written, threatening messages he'd left in some of the old cabins on the lake.

Jay Hammond gives a first-hand account of Billy in his book, *Bush Rat Governor*: "As lethal a creature as I've ever encountered" and "tough as a wolverine. And like a wolverine, what Billy couldn't consume, he'd rip apart or defile."

Why we never felt we were in danger I'm not sure. Maybe Billy was just one more thing in a totally foreign world we were trying to accept and enter. Anyway, he was invisible, possibly there but never seen, just like the long-tailed cat that supposedly frequented the area's volcanoes and the yeti that local people swore they'd spotted.

When Molly joined me at Lake Becharof later that summer, she took the mail plane from King Salmon to Egegik. There was only one other passenger on the plane—yes, Crazy Billy. He never said a word to her, maybe because he was known to be quite deaf and not much given to conversation. Molly and Billy parted ways once they stepped out on the Egegik airstrip.

Alaska summers were short, salmon were starting to show up in the subsistence nets set along the beach, and the high tides so critical for our trip up the river were building. It was time to start our project. Howie and I (Molly had yet to join us) borrowed an old setnet skiff and motor from a generous man who sold outboard engines, bought enough food for a few months from Alaska Packers Cannery, packed up a case of beer, and gladly took the offer of a tow behind Jackie Abluma's gillnetter up the twenty-five-mile-long river.

With our loaded skiff tied to the stern of the bigger and more powerful boat, we departed one June morning on an incoming twenty-foot tide. "Riding the flood," we got a powerful boost up the river as the tide from the ocean pushed its way inland and increased our speed by several knots.

Gradually the river narrowed and began to look more like a river should, the tide slackened, the banks got higher, and we could see low hills. Jackie managed to run the boat up on a bar about fifteen miles from Egegik at a place called the First Lagoon. Since the tide was going out, we had no choice but to wait twelve hours to be floated off. More than a mile wide and several miles long, the lagoon was like a lake. The only feature we could see was a narrow spit of land sticking out into the water. As we sat—high and dry, as mariners say—Jackie told us about the ghost of a woman who disappeared on the spit years ago that appears from time to time picking berries.

We floated off the bar on the next tide and motored to and across the Second Lagoon, to where the tidal influence stopped and the river ran free and clear. We anchored the valuable and deep-drafted gillnetter at the bottom of a series of shallow rapids and climbed into the smaller flat-bottomed skiff, Jackie at the helm. Slowly we pushed our way up the river in our underpowered, overloaded boat. House-sized boulders and white water passed with agonizing slow-ness; the river was steep enough that from the boat all you could see was water coming down at you, and over that a narrow ribbon of gray sky. There was no visibility beyond a few yards in front of us. One minute I was questioning whether we'd make it, and the next we burst out onto a huge peaceful lake.

We motored a few hundred yards to a sandy beach and Jackie got out. To this day I can see him standing on the shore waving to us, and then turning, rifle in hand, and disappearing over a hill as he walked back toward his boat. We weren't to see him again for six weeks when we went back to Egegik to pick up Molly.

In those days I never had any money. A few years later I would have had a research grant from this place or that. I would have chartered a plane and flown survey flights and previewed all that I'd see on the ground. I would have had the latest equipment, a resupply schedule, and my research would have taken priority over everything else. We would have radio communication with some-one should we need help. And I would be in a hurry to get on with my data collection—to make sure I had the information to finish my degree.

But that summer we came into the country without hurry or urgency—slowly and gently. And I'm glad we did. Talking to Dea-con on the beach, hearing about bears from people in Egegik, going through the rapids, waving goodbye to Jackie . . . all these moments gave me a feeling for the place I still have today.

Howie and I really did slow down to what we used to jokingly call Aleutian Standard Time—a time when ghosts might exist and when there were plenty of hours for rest and dreaming.

# TWO

## LAKE BECHAROF

# 6

## First Bear

**L**ake Becharof lies east and west on the Alaska Peninsula. If it weren't for the Aleutian Mountains, which run north and south at the eastern end, the lake and river would cut the peninsula in half. As it is, a walk of a few hours through the mountains brings you to Shelikof Strait where you can see Kodiak Island some forty miles away.

The western part of the lake, the part closest to Bristol Bay, the Egegik River, and the rapids, lies in a mostly flat coastal plain. The more rolling and mountainous land of the eastern end is where most of the inlet streams and rivers are located. The lake is about thirty-five miles long and up to fifteen miles wide. When you look out from the top of the rapids, eastward down the lake, you see the top half of 3,000-foot mountain peaks sticking up in a jagged line out of the water. Looking south, you see Mount Peulik, a 4,835-foot classic, smoking, steep-sided volcano. On a clear day, the mountain is never out of sight from anywhere on the lake, which is handy because volcanoes need lots of watching.

Halfway down the lake, on the southern shore, are two 500-foot rock hills known as Gas Rocks, named for the continuous silver bubbles that stream up from the bottom of the lake just in front of them. They are doubtless connected to nearby Mount Peulik. In fact, in 1977 two large volcanic vents named Ukinrek Maars opened in the tundra between Gas Rocks and Mount Peulik.

These features weren't there in 1966. But Gas Rocks rose dramatically on the lakeshore and dwarfed the nearby low alder-covered hills. We had been told several times by people in Egegik to head for Gas Rocks and stop and check the weather there. The rocks and nearby island offered the only shelter from the super power-ful southeast winds.

Our goal, the goal of most of the Bristol Bay red salmon, and hope-fully the goal of lots of brown bears, was to end up at the streams at the far end of the lake.

It was an obvious straight shot down the lake. The water was calm, but because we had been warned winds can come up quickly, we placed Gas Rocks over the bow and headed for the silver bubbles. We'd also heard about a nearby island where sea monsters rested, an eternally frozen waterfall that lay somewhere in the mountains near Shelikof Strait, and the long-tailed Peulik cats, which lived on the slopes of Mount Peulik.

Picture two guys in a boat, alone on a huge lake, with four drums of gas, two months' worth of food, thousands of feet of unexposed film, and all the time in the world. Time really did slow, miles meant little, and we focused on wind, wave size, and clouds. Meals hap-pened when we were hungry (always), days lasted until sleep, and we seldom talked—Howie was renowned for his long silences—and we both thought our own thoughts.

When we reached Gas Rocks, we admired the bubbles and two bull moose on the shore. We tossed a Sailor Boy Pilot Cracker into the water—they come in a blue box with a sailor boy on it and never go bad—for the sea monster. I still do this each time I pass.

The weather held, the motor still worked, and we continued down the lake in flat, calm water that reflected a peaceful sky, something we were soon to learn seldom occurred in that country.

Then, about five miles past Gas Rocks we saw two bears walking on the lakeshore. I stopped the engine, and we drifted until we were about a hundred yards from them. Perhaps sensing us, they turned, climbed the steep bank, and disappeared into a big patch of alders.

Looking back at these the first brown bears I had ever seen, I see myself as I was then, young, in shape, no responsibilities, and no phone or radio. I could totally concentrate on the moment, in this case the two bears. There was no need to talk or explain, and I don't know what Howie was thinking. We both sat and stared at the spot where the bears had disappeared.

That short experience with the two bears is etched in my memory. Two light-colored, lanky bears walk on a rocky beach. Howie and I sit in a battered gray skiff, close to the bears, which are looking at us. Mount Peulik smokes in the background, the sky is an eastern Montana sky, going on forever and ever. Lake Becharof is deep blue and without a ripple. We watch as the bears walk silently on broad padded feet. There is no sound.

I wrote these notes at about one the next morning. It was a very long day.

July 1, 1966

Two bears were observed at 9 p.m. five or six miles below Gas Rocks. They were first seen about a mile away. Both appeared to be the same size. My guess is they were young bears. One was regular brown in color the other much lighter. The bears were on the lakeshore when first seen and disappeared going up the [lake] bank and into the alders. Both bears departed together. Both seemed compatible, in fact no thought was given that things might be otherwise.

I could have gone ashore and followed them, but I wasn't sure what the bears would tolerate—or what I could. I already had in my mind that I would like to follow a mother with cubs for a few weeks, but at this point I was but a babe myself when it came to bear behavior.

I had not read about anyone else following free-ranging bears to learn about maternal behavior. It is possible someone had but I had missed the reference. Perhaps the bear followers weren't writers. Regardless, I had no one to emulate.

It was twilight as we passed through the Big Narrows, a place where the lake narrows to about a half mile before opening up again into Island Lake, which as the name implies is full of small islands. About a mile from the narrows, we easily located a cabin called Norwegian Home. It stuck out conspicuously in a country where the highest vegetation seldom grows more than fifteen to twenty feet high. Norwegian Home was once a popular stopping-off place between Egegik on the Bering Sea and the now-abandoned town of Kanatak on Shelikof Strait. For thousands of years people traversed the Alaska Peninsula here, not only as they moved from the western side and then on over to Kodiak, but also as they moved from harvesting salmon in the summer to land mammals in the fall. Now the cabin was used while hunting and for simply getting out of town. We made ourselves at home as our friends in Egegik said we should.

The two-room cabin was remarkably sound and we were pleased to see it had a wood stove. Scattered around outside we found large mammal bones—either moose or horse, we couldn't tell—along with a horse collar and several pairs of ice skates.

I stood inside and from the window of the cabin I could see the mouth of Featherly Creek, a clear stream that I'd noted on the maps. We spotted red salmon swirling off the stream mouth. Even before unpacking and having something to eat, I waded a mile or so up the creek. No dead salmon, crushed grass, or sign that the trails bordering the creek had been recently used. Even in my naivete, it looked to me as if the bears hadn't been around yet. The only activity in the area being the mass of fish off the bar at the stream's mouth.

Today I have a good idea where the bears were on that early summer evening, although it would take me a long time to make educated guesses about the movements and migrations of Alaska Peninsula bears. But right then I didn't have a clue, except I was pretty sure I wasn't in the right place and my proposed bear study would fizzle.

Then, after two days and more than twenty hours of watching, a medium-sized male bear appeared walking down the lakeshore and entering the water right off the stream mouth. Within an hour he had caught three fish. He'd chase fish until one got into shallow water, descend on it bodily, and eventually grab the struggling salmon out of the water with his mouth. Each time he caught a fish, the bear disappeared into the alders with his catch. I sat entranced, watching all this with the aid of a spotting scope from about a hundred yards. This was the second time in my life I'd seen a brown bear— and the first time I'd seen a bear catch a salmon.

At this point I was lacking two very important ingredients of my bear study. One was the behavior of salmon, and the other was correct observation technique for bears. I was not altogether clueless and had read lots of literature about red salmon, but I knew nothing about the particular fish that lived in Lake Becharof, most notably when and where they spawned. I knew the Fish and Game hoped for a million-fish escapement (that's the number of fish needed for reproduction) into the lake and that the run peaked in salt water, where commercial fishing was allowed, around the Fourth of July.

I didn't know much about the bears of Becharof, but I did know I wanted to watch bears being bears. So I kept my distance, sitting in the same place hour after hour, waiting for him to show up, rather than going out and exploring the countryside. The classical ethological approach I'd embraced demanded I keep interaction to a minimum. That's what I did in those first days and that's what I still practice today.

I watched the Featherly Creek bear as he fished for three to four hours a day for three days. He was the only bear that showed up. A moon-shaped scar over his left eye identified him, and Howie named him Chocolate George for his dark brown coat. Using a long telephoto, Howie took pictures, however we both realized we'd have to get much closer to get the best images.

As the fish seemed hesitant to leave the lake and enter the stream and there was only one bear, we eventually decided to start exploring. We packed a tent and some food into the skiff and headed eastward toward the complex of streams that ran down out of the mountains. It was at this eastern end of the lake that we spent most of the rest of that season and all of the next two. We did go back to Norwegian Home and Featherly Creek once the salmon entered the creek, but we'd realized it wasn't the best place to watch bears. The steeper gradients and broken ground cover of the mountains and foothills to the east proved to be far better.

As we passed through the islands that give Island Lake its name, we immediately began to see bears on the hillsides above the shore. I had never dreamed brown bears could be so abundant. I counted at least forty. As soon as we could, we ran the skiff up on a sandy beach and began to watch what was to be a never-ending show.

My journal entry for the day is a bit confused. I had never anticipated I'd be seeing so many bears at once. I tried to describe each bear and their activities. Scarcely the stuff of great science, but it was a beginning:

Bears 7, 8, 9

Light brown female with two large cubs. Feeding on hillside 200 yards away.

Bear 10

Large dark bear only seen for a moment 75 yards away. Stood up and faced us while we were photographing bear family 7, 8, 9.

Bear 11

[Written in camp. Taken from my field notes.] Howie has named the creek Scare Creek. He was photographing family 7, 8, 9. I was watching through my spotting scope but saw the new bear as he walked down the lakeshore toward the boat. He apparently noticed me when I poked Howie. A moment of looking by all hands. The bear continued to move forward crossing the stream coming directly toward us. He stopped at 20 paces, backed up a few steps, quickly turned, and took off running. He stopped about 50 yards away again facing toward us. Appeared to be a small young bear.

Bears 12, 13, 14

On lakeshore. Mother is huge and brown and easily recognized. Two cubs of the year. Moving at a fast walk, upwind from us. Cubs follow closely while female leads. One cub is nudged when it tried to pass her, the other picked up a stick and carried it two steps. In sight for 15 minutes.

Two days later I was pleased that I could differentiate two females with yearlings and three with cubs of the year.

Howie was already picking and choosing what scenes and bears he wanted to film. I was working on making positive identifications, writing down activities, watching for interactions, and was about as happy as I'd ever been.

We didn't want to disturb our prey on the mainland and were definitely still unsure of our social impact, so we camped on one of the islands about 150 yards off what we now called Scare Creek. One hundred and fifty yards is a long distance, and I soon learned that bears will tolerate you much closer. Though I erred on the side of caution, these early observations made while anchored a short distance from shore in the skiff and from the island gave me some of the best information I have ever gathered about how bears spend their days.

I watched bears walking and waiting on the beaches, seemingly in anticipation of the time the salmon would become vulnerable in the streams.

I watched bears in the open tundra as they grazed, slept, nursed, and dug for Arctic ground squirrels (*Urocitellus parryii*) and Arctic lupine (*Lupinus nootkatensis*) taproots.

I routinely spotted twenty or more bears. Sometimes I was able to keep track of the same bear for six or eight hours. I couldn't really identify individuals as I was too far away, but I did start to understand how bears spent the twenty-odd hours of daylight in early summer. I watched for days on end—bears going about the business of being bears, without any impact from me.

As well as writing descriptive notes, I recorded "scans" of everything I saw during fifteen-minute periods. I tried to do this every hour on the hour. Here's an example:

July 4, 1966, from Island

Scan: 12 to 12:15 p.m.

Family A [female and two yearlings] feeding in foreground. Uphill from them Family B [female and three yearlings]. Family E [female and three cubs of the year] is nursing—2 minutes—150 yards from B. Two small bears traveling together appear out of alders near Bear Creek. Single bear moving toward Family B.

Scan: 3 to 3:15 p.m.

Been watching Family B for two hours. Same locale as 12 p.m. Eating something that requires tearing up tundra. At one point [smelled something?] mother stopped eating and ran with cubs about 20 yards. Stood up. Returned to where she'd been eating. Cubs close and stood twice as much as mother. At times cubs stood up with front paws against her. Cubs chased gulls several times. Excavation is now big enough for all four bears to get into. Looks about a foot deep.

Scan: 4 to 4:15 p.m.

From Island. Family E [mother and 3 cubs of the year] came over
ridge at the exact spot they had gone out of sight. Walked to within
50 yards of Family B who are still digging and feeding. Mother E
stopped and faced the B's for a moment and then proceeded toward
them down a gully and out of sight. [Reappeared] moving away from
B's. She is bigger than mother B but her cubs are smaller. All of this
going on with another mother and two yearlings grazing 200 yards
away, not paying other bears attention. Cubs look like yearling, certainly not cubs of the year. Everyone is brown. [Brown bears!] Could
be Family D. Hard as hell to tell everyone apart.

I began to figure out how I would be able to follow a mother and
cubs at a closer distance, something I still very much wanted to do.

Watching an animal that you are unsure of isn't the easiest thing.
I honestly didn't know what I would do if a big old bear walked up
to me. It took quite a bit of learning and I was making up my own
rules as I went along. Remember, I'm a self-taught bear watcher.

In those days I always carried a 12-gauge shotgun—there was no
such thing as bear spray. I had never talked to anyone who had sat
in the open for long periods with bears. I knew the Craigheads did
much of their Yellowstone observations from vehicles. Andy Russell's book, *Grizzly Country*, and his accounts of being close to and
approached by bears wouldn't be published for another year.

After a week or so staying on the island, we again packed up the
boat and headed southeast ten miles to the far end of the lake. Here
we found a few old houses in a place called Fish Village. People from
Egegik and winter residents of the lake used to come here in the fall
and catch spawning Arctic char and, I would guess, burbot, in the
shallow water. One house was in good shape and evidently used by
bear hunters according to notes in a guestbook left on a table. Howie
and I figured there might be some bad karma because of the possible
associated bear killing, but were grateful to sleep under a good roof.

We also found a copy of the adventure magazine *Saga Man* left
behind. From then on, whenever one of us performed a particular heroic deed, such as fixing the outboard engine or washing the
dishes in the rain, we'd give each other various "Saga Man" awards.

During these first two months on Lake Becharof, we never saw
another soul.

# 7

# A Dance of Displeasure

You can do the best science in the world, but unless emotion is involved, it's not really very relevant. Conservation is based on emotion. It comes from the heart and one should never forget that.

—George Schaller

owie, Molly, and I spent the summer and fall of 1966 at Lake Becharof. Sitting today in Homer in a warm house, I have to try hard to remember how cold and wet we often were. Life with morning frosts and weeklong storms blowing in from Shelikof Strait to the east or Bristol Bay to the west couldn't have always been pleasant. The wind and rain at Becharof funnels through and over the Aleutian Mountains and slams down onto the waters at the eastern end of the lake, making waterspouts common. I went out every day in spite of the weather, although sometimes it was late in the afternoon before I left the shelter of "Jake's Cabin," as people from Egegik called the small cabin we came to occupy.

Even summer months on the Alaska Peninsula can make for hard living. Our raingear snagged on errant alder branches and rubber boots leaked from miles of walking. Somehow, we managed to eat the best store-bought foods first, giving way to a monotonous diet of Dolly Varden trout and Arctic grayling. However, things would brighten up in the fall with changing colors, fried ptarmigan at dinner, and blueberry pancakes for breakfast.

One staple, always available, was instant mashed potatoes. Howie, who never worried about such mundane things as eating, once purchased two cases of #10 cans—that comes to twelve cans and perhaps twenty pounds of dried potatoes—enough for at least a lifetime. Even opened these cans pretty much last forever, and if left exposed to air generate a barrier of mold that protects the dry potatoes underneath. There always seemed to be an open can around—just add water to hydrate, and maple syrup to mask the cardboard taste.

By fall the bears were fat and what had been small scrawny spring cubs were now 150-pound-plus butterballs. Bear coats that had been sun-bleached, rubbed in spots to expose under hair, and ultimately shed during the summer had grown into spectacular new coats, giving the bears a glossy, fluid look. A bull moose has his annual antlers, and a fall bear has a new coat that it is too often killed for.

When I think of killing a bear just to hang its hide on the wall, the words of an unknown author come to mind. He or she prefaced Alexander Pope's lines—"Know, nature's children all divide her care; / The fur that warms a monarch, warm'd a bear."—with "Beware, Beware."

What I learned in those years at Becharof has become the foundation of what I know of bears today. I have to laugh at how long it took and how much time I wasted divesting myself of the emotional baggage and preconceived notions I took into the field.

However, if I could do it all again, relive those first years and first bears, I wouldn't do things differently. I got over my fears, sharpened up my objectivity, and today feel most of my observations and data collected have stood the test of time. I had no teacher, save what I read. Having George Schaller and Niko Tinbergen as guiding influences was paramount to my success. Molly listened and helped clarify my thoughts. The Becharof bears proved to be incredible and complex animals revealing parts of their lives to me as I watched.

It seems odd but today I can't clearly remember the first bear that approached me. I know it happened that summer. In my mind's eye, there's a glimmer of a bear walking over to me for no apparent reason, not stopping at fifty feet then slowly turning and walking off as most did, but rather approaching and appearing to look me over from just a few feet away. This was a different bear from the one that a few days earlier let me sit nearby on a stream bank as it patiently fished. This was one that came up as I was sitting alone on the tundra, notebook in hand, stopping only when I stood up and said, "Close enough." An instruction that came naturally and appears to be well enough understood by both bears and myself that I have continued to use it over the years.

For me, the approaching bear was never a moment of truth, or a test of bravery. It was just something I knew I'd have to learn how to do if I was to study bears. Today when a bear approaches to seemingly check me out, my pulse sometimes races. I still prefer close encounters not to happen, but I have learned enough to understand bears are individuals and usually have good reason for interacting with me.

I learned the best way to watch was to sit where bears came to feed. It helped to pick a distance the bears would tolerate and to choose a regular, specific place they were used to seeing me. The bears took care of the rest. This all took time; my relaxed attitude didn't happen overnight. I had to learn and believe—believing and self-convincing being the hard part—that something else besides mayhem was going on beyond those dark, impenetrable eyes.

That first summer I had established a trail—actually making use of one made by bears—on Cleo Creek at the eastern end of the lake. From the trail I could see different sections of the stream and discovered there was a limit, marked by a small waterfall, to how far upstream the salmon swam and spawned. The length of the creek, from the outlet at the lake to the waterfall a few miles upstream, became my study area. Every morning and evening I'd walk its length. Some days, once the salmon entered the creek and staked out spawning redds or beds, they were easy prey, and I'd count as many as fifteen bears catching and eating. On these walks, I began to learn and collect information on play behavior, as it seemed once the bears filled up on salmon, they'd move out into open areas and perform. Some days Howie would come with me and film the parade of bears and salmon, at other times he'd disappear out onto the lake or into the mountains to take footage of other parts of the incredible world we were part of.

I was always aware of the possibility of meeting bears as I walked. I had lots to learn. However, it didn't take me long to realize that for the most part bears walked up and down the creek either in the water or on continuous trails on each bank. When bears moved in and out of the area, they tended to walk at right angles to the creek. If I stayed where there was good visibility, away from bear trails, I could usually see the bears before they got close and moved away from me. From the onset, it was never about meeting bears and reporting their reactions—though I did this. More importantly, I tried to simply be a part of the landscape and minimize any effect I might have.

I was amazed to find most bears didn't seem to be bothered by my watching them. However, one huge dark male, who we called Monarch the Big Bear (MBB for short) after the bear in Ernest Thompson Seton's book, wanted nothing to do with me, running away whenever he noticed me. Another big male named Slade, whom you met in the introduction, tolerated me but sometimes seemed to give me hard looks as he faced in my direction. Others, particularly mothers and cubs, and what I was pretty sure were subadults, seemingly paid little attention.

The best place to watch was at the mouth of Cleo Creek. When we got to this end of the lake, there were fish off the creek but not in the creek proper. A big red mass—the salmon having changed from their oceangoing silver to their spawning colors—hung out in the deep water just off a shallow sandbar where they would later become vulnerable to bears. It was hard to estimate how many fish there were—five, ten, twenty thousand? We never knew. However, we did know the streams in this part of Becharof were the most productive on the lake.

The schooling salmon splashed as they swirled and waited—for what I'm not sure—water level and temperature, turbidity, changes in their reproductive condition? The splashing attracted bears walking the beaches. Some bears would make futile dives in attempts to capture fish. However—and here we get to see what a bear is— very few bears could dive into the mass and come up with a fish. That some bears did this and others did not gave me an inkling that bears were not peas in a pod or identical flowers in the field. These bears did not pin fish to the bottom, a common fishing technique in shallow streams, but rather grabbed them in their mouths in ten to twenty feet of water.

One day in July, at the height of the salmon run, Molly and I left Jake's Cabin and headed south along the lakeshore for about a mile to the mouth of Cleo Creek. We came prepared to watch bears until late evening with lots of food, warm clothes, and raingear. We looked upstream before crossing to make certain we wouldn't surprise any bears, and quickly made our way over to Hammond's cabin, a long-abandoned, flat-roofed, doorless, and windowless shack, about a hundred feet from the creek bank.

Using an old gas drum as a ladder, we climbed onto the roof. I left Molly here for a few hours to see what bears were around and took off for my daily walk to the waterfall at the top of the creek, count-ing and identifying bears along the way. When I got back we spent the rest of the day taking notes and enjoying not having to worry about bears walking up behind us.

Around 9:30 p.m. the sun dropped toward the horizon. The shad-ows deepened as the islands on the lake blocked the light to the west, and we decided it was time to go home. The procedure to do so was simple. Wait until all the bears were out of sight or eating recently caught fish, climb down from the roof, quickly cross the creek, then walk up the lakeshore to our cabin.

We waited until the coast was clear and started across the creek, only to have a midsized male come running down the creek in hot pursuit of a fleeing salmon. In its haste to escape, the fish shot between Molly and myself. The bear never looked up until I yelled, "Hey, bear!" when it got within fifteen feet from us. The bear came to a halt, but instead of apologetically stopping, turning, and going back upstream or making a detour around us, he began a dance of displeasure.

Needless to say, we gave the bear all our attention and slowly backed away, with the intent of increasing the distance between us and the now salivating bear. He reacted to our movement by turning broadside to us with lowered head, ears back, and mouth open—all classic aggressive signals I was all too aware of having observed them in bear-to-bear encounters.

We continued to slowly back up, eventually putting about twenty-five feet between us and the bear. At this point he began to make popping noises, a particular sound that agitated bears make using their teeth and cheeks.

We continued to back up but apparently the bear seemed to think this was the right distance between us—as we backed, he closed the distance. His movements slowed and he began what we later called "cowboy walking"—a stiff-legged, open-mouthed, head-lowered display, made up of short steps and urination. I did not look to see if this particular male was peeing.

Cowboy walking can be an end in itself if an adversary moves or signals submission, but it might lead to any number of things, one of which is an increase and continuation of aggressive behavior. He abruptly quit the swaggering postures and turned laterally to us, zigzagging for short distances, only coming toward us when we moved back—and move back we did, right to the lake, then out into the lake, then to the top of my hip boots, then my waist, then Molly climbed up on my shoulders, and it was either swim or make our way around the bear who by this time was doing nothing more than standing in the shallows watching us.

I'd like to say we remained cool, calm, and collected, with no stress or racing pulses. In reality, we were just as scared as most anyone would have been after having five hundred pounds of bear displaying at them in an aggressive manner. Up to that time I'd never had a bear behave like this toward me.

Then it ended. As we were deciding what to do, still standing waist-deep in the lake, the bear turned around, walked back upstream, and disappeared. I like to think when Molly got on my shoulders we turned into a giant nine-foot bear dressed in green raingear and we intimidated the bear. Now I think when we stopped retreating, the game of "you move and I'll move" ended and the bear lost interest or perhaps thought he had successfully dominated us. Now I know standing your ground is the best thing to do with an aggressive bear if increasing your distance doesn't work. I also know now that the best way to encourage a bear to follow you is to move away from it.

That should be the end of this bear story, except after we got back to shore and dumped the water out of our hip boots and began to head up the beach, I noticed movement about a hundred feet away on the top of an old beach berm. The light was fading but it sure looked like the same bear. Whoever it was kept his distance but paralleled us on our mile-long trip to the cabin, moving silently but giving himself away by occasionally becoming a silhouette against a darkening sky.

• • •

No two days were the same at Lake Becharof. A new bear could appear, a caribou or moose might walk by on the beach, a flower bloom, or ptarmigan chicks hatch. One memorable day we surprised and filmed five bears and two wolverines eating a moose carcass. Occasionally, we'd spot a wolf and we'd often hear them at night as they called to each other.

There are no typical days in "bush" Alaska unless you stay in your cabin or tent and drink coffee and read. Both are worthy pursuits, but not a good way to learn about the landscape and bears. So, on a rainy fall day with the wind blowing from the southeast at thirty with gusts to forty miles per hour, Howie and I decided to leave the comforts of home and explore the upper reaches of Bear Creek to see how far upstream the salmon spawned.

I can only guess at the wind speed, as we never had a radio or weather report; however, when the rain stings your eyes it's generally above forty miles per hour. One cannot consider the physical aspects of place without including the wind. On Lake Becharof the wind seldom stops. It funnels through the mountain pass to the east—the one that leads to the old town site of Kanatak on Shelikof Strait—takes a right hand turn after mixing with the southern wind blowing up along the mountain front and the lower Alaska Peninsula, then rages up along the lakeshore and tries to knock you flat.

We were wet in the first twenty minutes of what ended up being an eight-hour hike. We didn't get hypothermic, why I'm uncertain, but kept moving to keep warm—I was a far, far tougher guy in those days. I often wonder whether Howie's ultimate disappearance at Lake Becharof wasn't caused by hypothermia. He had absolutely no fear of the elements.

My diary of the Bear Creek hike mentions it was "nasty" weather. We hiked three or four miles up to the top of the creek and a steep canyon where salmon and the usual accompanying bears and bear signs were absent. Evidently, there was better spawning habitat and easier fishing downstream. Our question about how far upstream the salmon spawned was answered.

We climbed a nearby mountain slope and plotted out our route back to the lakeshore. With the mountains behind us, the lake in front, there was no way to get lost, but we still looked for the easiest way down as walking through alder patches can be difficult. Alders can grow up to twenty feet high and if they are old can be eight to ten inches at the base. Open muskeg bogs where visibility is good and walking easier makes for a better path. The route we picked went down the hill we were on to a prominent ridge, along the length of the ridge, across a slope, and then down again to yet another ridge that ended at the lakeshore. As the light disappeared we stood for a moment concentrating, trying to memorize where the openings in the alder patches were. Howie was a giant slalom racer in college, and because he once memorized gates on a ski course he was usually pretty good at remembering trails, but by this time it was 10 p.m. and the light was poor. We set out picking our way as best we could—naturally walking on bear trails, as it's pretty hard at Lake Becharof to go any distance without being on one of these paths, as every ridge has a bear trail along the top, every valley has a trail at the bottom, every salmon stream has trails on both banks.

I was in the lead when suddenly a bear went crashing off into the alders a short distance in front of me. It makes you jump when they do this. If you want to know how strong a bear is, find a stand of mature alders, get a running start, and see how far you can get—it won't be very far. A terrified bear can smash through them as if they weren't there. You have to weave under and over, while a bear simply goes through—branches either bend or break. I'm sure we waited for a while before proceeding, only to discover the bear had come from the first in a series of bear beds that lined the ridge we were descending and which overlooked the best fishing area on Bear Creek. Several times in the next half hour, we surprised and scared bears that went crashing off. None ran over us.

We made it home by midnight—another eventful day at Lake Becharof. The significance of this story, this walk with Howie, other than I can still remember it, was all about finding the bear beds along the ridge, some over a mile from the creek, adding to my information about what bears do and where they go when they aren't fishing. It took me a while to learn that mothers with cubs as well as single females tend to bed up a good distance from the streams when not fishing, leaving the alders next to the water for larger males. It was also a lesson in why not to walk ridgelines near salmon streams on dark and stormy nights.

# 8

## Now I Understand—Social Bears

The year 1967 was terrible for the country. I had relaxed in Vermont and Alaska thanks to my student deferment while my two best friends—men with whom I had shared twelve years of school, gotten drunk, raced cars, discovered girls, and hunted—were in Vietnam. Both were wounded and later heavily decorated for their valor.

I was very much opposed to the war, and didn't want to go. But I volunteered for the draft to see what would happen, and for various medical reasons the army said it only wanted me if it was a national emergency. Vietnam wasn't considered one. Instead, it was a national tragedy. I was off the hook and never had to confirm my beliefs with my actions. I'm still haunted today.

I was fortunate enough to spend months in a wild, natural world away from newspapers, radio broadcasts, and television images of a horrible time.

May 27, 1967

Left Egegik at 3 a.m. on 20-foot tide. Made it to the Fish and Game Cabin [situated just below the rapids] in three hours. Split up the load and made three trips through the rapids. The boat contained among other things 170 gallons of gas, oil, tools to repair uncooperative motors, a portable generator, over 1,000 pounds of food and equipment, an extra motor, and three people. [Our motor wasn't capable of pushing the boat with the complete load up the rapids. Gas alone weighed 1,400 pounds.] Reloaded the boat after a meal and went an hour east in windy weather. Decided to split the load in half for safety's sake. Made a cache on shore and slept for an hour. 4 hours sleep in 48. Made it to Gas Rocks in three hours through three-foot waves. Set up tents and slept for 12 hours. Wind switched from SE to SW. Saw a caribou. Made it to Norwegian Home in Island Lake in three hours. Very windy and were only able to make progress [in a very overloaded skiff] going downwind crossing over to Jake's. Found cabin in mess [from fall moose hunters]. Ate supper and climbed hill behind camp to look for bears. Saw two big bull moose. Set up tent [a clean tent is always preferable to a dirty cabin]. Falling asleep. A large animal went by. [Too tired to care.] Footprints next day showed two moose and one large bear.

In late May of 1967, Molly, Howie, and I began our second summer at Becharof. Using the same weathered skiff of the previous year, we traveled from Egegik to the old cabin at the eastern end of the lake, covering the seventy miles of river and lake in two long days.

This was to be the last year of my bear investigations needed to complete my Goddard thesis titled "An Ethologist Looks at *Ursus arctos.*" We planned to stay until the middle of October, leaving before bear-hunting season, an event we didn't want to experience.

In this second year my research goals included gathering more data on social interactions and following mothers and cubs when opportunities were presented. I also wanted to spend as much time as possible with fishing bears on Cleo Creek, further identifying communicative signals and describing social organization.

Now in late May the last remnants of winter were still visible around Lake Becharof, with snow patches dotting the mountain-sides, vegetation still brown, and few bears. We had the whole lake to ourselves. People from Egegik who might have come up to visit were busy getting ready for fishing season.

Jake's Cabin, the one we had moved into the previous July, like Norwegian Home, appears very much alone when you approach by boat, rising abruptly in high grasses about fifty feet from the lakeshore, behind a narrow beach. Built with rough-cut lumber the ten-by-sixteen-foot structure had a metal roof that didn't leak, a woodstove we could cook on, and a Douglas fir floor made of old four-by-twelve-inch planks likely salvaged from one of the huge Bristol Bay salmon canneries built in the early part of the last century.

We settled quickly into the cabin, which was sparsely furnished but extensively decorated with roughly scissored cutouts of the black-hatted Quaker Oats man thumbtacked to the walls. Evidently, past inhabitants had an abundance of both cereal and spare time.

Jake's faced due west, so when the weather was clear we stood by the front door and viewed midnight sunsets through the off-shore islands. To the east behind the cabin, low hills and muskeg swamps gave way to the rugged mountains of the Aleutian Range.

Before we had left Egegik, Deacon's wife told us that if need be we could borrow the relatively new woodstove from their cabin on the lake. Later, I realized she knew she and Deacon wouldn't be returning. Our stove was in sorry shape so in a day or two we crossed the lake to get theirs. Posted on the door was a crudely scrawled "Keep Out." Crazy Billy Nekeferoff had gotten there first. But the stove was still there and, unfazed, we packed it out.

The gravel beaches on this part of the lake served as bear highways. Jake's Cabin sat a few feet from the beach, and when we were there we learned from looking at their tracks that bears would walk along the beach until they got within a short distance of the cabin and then make a detour, passing inland behind the building before looping back to the shore and continuing on their way north or south. Of the many bears that went by, only a handful ever walked in front of the cabin.

I don't know why the bears avoided the cabin. Loathing? Fear? Trepidation? Good manners?

Another bear trail ran along the low ridge just a few hundred yards behind the cabin. When they didn't take the beach, bears used this as they walked between Cleo Creek to the south and Becharof Creek to the north. Some mornings when I'd stick my head out of the cabin door to check the weather, I'd spot a bear on this path dark against the sky. Sometimes bears would nose around the skiff, giving it careful examination. We soon learned to be careful when fueling the outboards. Bears always noticed spilled gas or oil and seemed to enjoy rubbing their bodies in it.

Because we didn't have a radio at Becharof, our weather forecasts were up to us. We'd look up and speculate as to what the weather was going to do that day. Notable at Becharof were the lenticular clouds. These lens-shaped clouds form at high attitudes and are frequently associated with moist air flowing over mountaintops, like those at our end of the lake. Mount Peulik creates them, too. I'd occasionally flip through *Silver Surfer* comic books someone had left in the cabin. The Silver Surfer, a super hero, saves the world by riding on a surfboard through the cosmos. Whenever those lenticulars appeared I thought they were beautiful and looked perfect for him to surf on, so they became "Silver Surfer clouds." Molly and I still call them that.

Like many of my fellow biologists and hunters, I've prepared for a day in the wild a thousand times. Get up at five or six, drink as much coffee as possible, eat as much oatmeal or granola as you can hold, dress for what you see out the window, and remember that the sunlight of the moment can rapidly turn into cold wind and rain. Temperatures might start at forty-five and climb to seventy-five as the sun warms things up or conversely start warm and dip to forty degrees.

Here's what I squeezed into my pack: raingear, something waterproof to sit on as the ground is usually damp, special yellow write-in-the-rain notebooks, data sheets, pencils, wool hats, gloves, camera gear, a first aid kit, binoculars, spotting scope, candy bars for snacks, several PB&Js for lunch, an apple if there were any left, water bottles, extra socks, head net, head lamp, mosquito repellent, sunscreen, matches, compass, emergency space blanket, and another clothing layer or two for when the wind picked up. At Becharof, because like the bears we were in and out of the water, we wore hip boots, switching to hiking boots for long hikes on dry terrain.

We took as much as we could manage to carry. Data collecting and filming were real jobs and human frailties should never interfere, despite getting cold, wet, and sunburned. I had a baseball hat that said "No Whiners," something we all strived not to be.

When we arrived the Bristol Bay red salmon run was still a month away and there were no fish in the streams. However, we were an optimistic crew and knew salmon would come and the bears would follow. There were still a few bears around and I spent days observing bear families, not long out of their dens, feeding on small patches of emerging plants. I'd slowly cruise the lakeshore in the skiff, spot some bears, go ashore, and find a good place to sit and watch.

There was little mating behavior during May and early June at Becharof, not so to the east along Shelikof, where it is common to see mating and high concentrations of bears. I didn't know this at the time. A few years later I learned about the phenomena of bears frequenting the coastal sedges. Since then I have visited the western beaches along Shelikof Strait every spring.

After a year in the field, I thought of myself as a real bearophile. According to my notes, by that point I could recognize seven different bear families, six single male and female bears, and two sets of small bears that traveled together. There were other bears around but these particular bears were regulars in my study area.

• • •

During that first year at Becharof, I documented more than five hundred encounters, or aggressive interactions, between bears. My definition for identifying an aggressive interaction or encounter was quite simple: "When one bear alters the ongoing behavior of another bear."

Looking at which bear was dominant or submissive in these interactions, I was able to identify which bears—at least those visiting the area between Bear and Cleo Creeks—lived within the confines of a "dominance hierarchy," a form of social structure maintained by aggressive displays.

Though some use it to describe hierarchies, I dislike the term "pecking order," because bears are not chickens. I sincerely doubt if Queen Elizabeth II referred to her subjects as being down in the pecking order. Another term for this social phenomenon, which occurs but varies within most species of animals, is "linear ranking."

Now, in this second summer, I continued to collect information, recording as many interactions as I could.

It's easy to do something when you're happy and I was really happy. This is what I wanted to do, and I didn't wish I was somewhere else. Keeping my focus and enthusiasm was never a problem and sitting and taking notes hour after hour was easy and a pleasure. The days were never long enough.

I'm preaching to the Alaskan choir, but when you're out by yourself, there is no one to listen to you gripe or complain. This is important. You get cold, you get up and walk around. You get tired, you find a place where you won't get stepped on and take a nap. If it rains or the wind blows too hard, you get under some alders or behind a rock. You carry lots of chocolate and save some coffee for the afternoon.

I just kept taking notes: A mother and cubs might be fishing in a stream with no other bears in sight. A big male approaches, ambling along the stream bank. She stops fishing and moves from the stream as he begins to fish in the same spot she had been using. I would record this as an aggressive encounter between a mother and cubs and a large male, noting she moved away from him and did not attempt to go back to where she had been feeding. During the course of the summer, I'd record every time females moved away from approaching big males. By October I had hundreds of examples and evidence that indeed large males were almost always dominant over females with cubs. In another example of dominant behavior, a large male, Bear A, is alternately lunching on a moose carcass and resting a few feet away. As he lies there, Bear B, another large male, approaches. A runs directly at him, B quickly turns, breaks into a run, and leaves the area.

I'd record this as an aggressive encounter between Bears A and B. I would note B ran from A and left the area. If I saw these two interact four or five times during the summer and A was always the more dominant, I'd have information supporting that a hierarchy existed.

Prior to my work at Becharof, the only study of social behavior in brown bears I knew of was Maurice Hornocker's at Yellowstone National Park in the early '60s. His research and conclusions gave me a solid starting point for my data collection and invaluable insight into what I was seeing.

One thing, however, separated his study from what I was trying to accomplish. Most of his data collection came from bears visiting the refuse dumps at Yellowstone. He recognized in his work that a constant food supply over an extended period of time may have altered some behavioral traits.

By contrast, the bears of Becharof had constant food—salmon, sedges, and preferred vegetation—and their nourishment spread out over time and space. Not so, the garbage bears of Yellowstone. When the bell rang, they ate. Jeffrey Nelson, who collected data for the Craigheads and Hornocker at Yellowstone, and later for me when I moved to McNeil River, told me that when the garbage trucks from lodges and campgrounds rattled down the road, bears would come out of the brush and be waiting for dinner as the backs of the trucks opened.

• • •

In my early research, I learned that the commonly held belief that bears were unpredictable was a myth. I'd found the opposite to be true—bears exhibited very predictable behavior toward each other and toward me. When I realized this, observing and interacting with them was possible.

Bears have a sophisticated social system. Bears can and do communicate with each other. People have told me a bear came up to them and did this or that. Almost always these folks, who have just had the scare of their lives, end their tale with "I know bears are so unpredictable." The bear appears unpredictable because the person doesn't have a clue as to what the bear is saying. Bears don't speak English. So they talk to you in their own language, which has more visual components, contains sounds inaudible to you, and relies far more on smell.

That first year I never witnessed an unpredictable bear—one who surprised me with an unexpected action. Not one single bear. Perhaps they lived somewhere else.

Because bears were predictable in their behavior, I quickly realized it was in my best interest to be predictable too. I began to walk the same trails, as I made my daily observations, and always sat in the same places above the creek, on gravel river bars, or in the tundra. I hoped bears would expect to find me in these places and not be frightened off to other areas.

Molly, Howie, and I brought with us to Becharof a love of animals, seclusion, and wild places. We each had our own life, goals, and beliefs, but from the beginning none of us wanted to scare bears. Intuitively, from the very first bear we met on the trail in 1966 and through all those next two years at Becharof, we kept interactions as calm and nonthreatening as possible. We did our absolute best to make every encounter we had positive for man, woman, and beast.

My thesis was developing.

I now viewed bears as members of a species that existed in close proximity to each other, lived within a social system, and had interactions that were both predictable and complex.

While bears didn't usually hang out together and didn't cooperate in life-sustaining hunts, I had learned they were often social with one another. They played, touched, licked, sniffed, and did all manner of social things.

This was not the stuff of solitary animals, which is how many people label bears. This was not the way solitary animals should behave. I knew from my reading that animals deemed solitary or asocial were usually species difficult to observe and which often ranged apart from others of their kind.

I knew the shape of a brown bear's social organization wasn't analogous to other species. Bears were social animals and not primates, canids, rodents, or whales—they were bears! I have never understood why humans want to force one species' social system into a shape like that of another. We humans don't like to be compared to other species. Try going into a bar and calling a belligerent drunk an animal. One exception was the uninformed Alaskan candidate for vice president who wanted to be known as fierce and pugnacious and called herself a "mama grizzly."

• • •

I never found any evidence that bears were territorial. Being territorial means keeping other members of your species away from a given area. Wolves and primates are territorial—bears aren't.

Bears, like people, share home ranges. This mutual use of land and resources is the basis for bear social behavior. Bears share places and abundant food supplies such as salmon, clams, sedge meadows, and berry patches.

A home range is a bit of the earth containing life requirements for a bear, such as a denning site, a mate, and food. Radio, GPS, and satellite collars work great for determining the size of home ranges. Millions of dollars and tens of thousands of hours have been spent on this valuable research.

Neither home range nor territoriality is to be confused with critical space or individual distance. Regardless of what it's called, there is an area around animals that, if entered, causes the animal to react. In the case of bears, this reaction can be dramatic. Individual distance is impossible to quantify into feet and inches; rather, it can be tied to an activity, perception, hormonal levels, adrenalin, reproductive condition, previous experience—the list is endless. One can only marvel at the adaptability, individuality, and breadth of behavior of brown bears as they defend or retreat when their individual distance is interrupted.

When you have entered a bear's critical space, you have forced the bear to act—either to move away or to be aggressive. The size of the critical space is different for every bear and situation.

Imagine you are in bear country hiking somewhere with limited visibility. Pretending you are either Davy Crockett or Daniel Boone, you move silently through the trees. You think saying "Hey bear, ho bear" ad nauseam is for scaredy-cats—not for true mountain men—so you walk silently. You round a corner in the trail and there lying in front of you is a mother bear with three cubs. Quicker than you ever thought possible, faster than the speed of light, she springs up and comes at you with an open-mouthed roar. In addition to surprising her, you have almost assuredly entered her personal space. Good luck.

· · ·

The social structure of Becharof bears looked like this: They lived in a hierarchy where mature males were at the top and subadults and cubs made up the bottom. Single females and females with cubs were submissive to mature males but had ranking within their own groups.

At the lowest rungs of the social ladder, not counting cubs still with their mothers, were single weaned two-and-a-half- and three-and-a-half-year-old subadults. Ranking slightly above them were sibling groups, young bears from the same litter that had stayed together and often acted as a unit to move other similar-sized bears from prime fishing spots and grazing areas. While it was difficult to say these sibs cooperated in aggressive encounters, frequently they approached other bears en masse.

I've had more than one interaction with sibling groups. No two encounters are the same; however, the young male in this bear story is indicative of a young animal finding its place in bear society. I have no doubt bears react to people much the way they react to other bears.

One August evening we headed back to the cabin after a day on Cleo Creek. For most of the day, Molly and I had watched bears we thought were siblings as they fished about a mile from the lakeshore. The male of the group repeatedly approached throughout the day, while the two females paid little attention other than turning toward us. The male's approaches had been slow and deliberate and he always stopped thirty or forty feet away.

I had no way of knowing if he was being curious or quite possibly asserting his dominance over us, puny humans that we were. I didn't even consider he was being predatory, although I probably should have.

As we made our way home, we came upon the three bears grazing and playing next to the trail. We stopped and waited, but as they showed no inclination to move we left the path and increased our distance to a degree we hoped would be acceptable to the bears. Evidently not far enough, as they stopped feeding and slowly moved in our direction. All we could do was stand our ground and wait.

When the bears were about fifty feet away, the two females stopped and faced us; the little male however acted differently. Unfortunately for him, I was pretty sure what he was up to—me being older and way more experienced than he was. After all his approaches I'd been expecting some sort of heightened aggression, so when he dropped his head and broke into a run directly toward us, I was ready and met his charge with my own, taking a few steps toward him and loudly saying, "Close enough." He immediately stopped, turned, and ran back to his sisters.

Perhaps he was testing me as he might another bear, possibly trying to assert his place within the Becharof hierarchy. After all, hierarchies are dynamic systems and a bear's social status changes with age and reproductive condition. There is a payoff for gaining position—the higher your social rank, the better your opportunities if food resources are limited and the better your chances to mate.

The slow dissolution of the bond that exists between female and offspring accounts for much of the social behavior I observed. This phenomenon of the bond, coupled with the fact that bears, particularly subadults as well as mature females, are likely making use of much the same home ranges as their mothers gives brown bear social organizations distinctly matriarchal overtones. Not matriarchal in that a female is the queen (although sometimes she can be) but rather she is a central figure.

Sometimes bears moved from stream to stream and would clump in groups along certain small sections rather than spread out. It got to the point we'd get up on late July mornings and say, "Where are the bears going to be today?"

Why? This could have been in response to environmental influences, but we didn't always get that feeling. Many days we'd find seven or eight recognizable bears—often comprised of several family groups—a few miles from where they had been the previous evening. Estimations of fish availability, stream flow or levels, and water turbidity gave no clue for the movement.

There were few mature males around so I didn't know how many were changing feeding spots. Of course, it's possible the domineering males we occasionally saw could have caused the females and cubs to relocate, as is often the case in other places.

In defense of scientific objectivity—I can see bear biologists rolling their eyes—without marking bears and using information gathered from DNA, my matriarchal theories were only theories. I didn't have the luxury of that kind of information. I'm still happy that one of the focal points of my three years at Lake Becharof was observing the behavior of mothers and cubs I got to know.

At Becharof it wasn't all about filling in data sheets or talking into a tape recorder. Just as important was sitting back and simply observing, looking for those events that helped me to define what a brown bear was.

# 9

## Becharof Days

The year was 1968. Martin Luther King was killed in April, Bobby Kennedy in early June, and the war dragged on. We just plain dropped out—perhaps irresponsibly—and by mid-June were back in the solitude of Lake Becharof. With no radio we never knew that Hubert Humphrey was going to run against Richard Nixon until we got back to Anchorage in mid-September.

I had finished my course work at Goddard, and my thesis was accepted. However, I wanted to collect more information on behavior and further explore the country. We had also become attached to living at Becharof. Nothing mystical or spiritual—Molly and I just liked it there, so we returned.

I loved the rainy days, the storms, yellow warblers displaying at each other, sandhill cranes nesting in the muskeg, foxes and moose looking at me, the strange gait of running caribou, grayling and trout waiting in the creeks for salmon eggs, ptarmigan families, beavers, otters, porcupines, fireweed, lupine, snowshoe hares, red-backed voles, Arctic ground squirrels, loons, frogs, shorebirds, cranes, ducks, swans . . .

That summer Howie and I spent more time filming than we had in other years. We had identified different places along salmon streams where we could see bears fishing and interacting with each other. Some days we'd go to these places, set up the camera, and wait. On others, particularly if it was cool and sitting for long periods was uncomfortable, we'd go out and look for bears.

Two mothers who had first-year cubs when we began, then yearlings the next year, now were alone and hopefully pregnant. The yearlings that were now two years old were hard to identify, as bears at this age can be extremely difficult to tell apart. I liked to imagine they were some of the subadults we saw almost every day.

Monarch had disappeared from the Cleo Creek area. Maybe he had enough of us and moved on, or possibly he had been killed in the past hunting season. He was a beautiful bear. We saw Slade on occasion but he seemed to prefer the bottom stretch of Bear Creek where visibility was limited. Cleo Creek appeared to be the home of younger bears and mothers and cubs.

Not a day passed when we didn't see bears.

### July 8, 1968

Molly's birthday! 22 years old and on her third year with bears. Salmon are starting to show up in numbers in Cleo Creek with many holding off the creek mouth. Some sunshine, maybe 55 degrees. We should bring a thermometer on next trip. Counting cubs, we saw 14 bears today. Female and 3 yearlings, female and 2 yearlings, female with 2 spring cubs in the distance. Single female of yesterday. Also 2 small bears and an unidentified young male. Jay Hammond flew in from Lake Clark with a father and son clients. They walked up Cleo and we had a pleasant conversation.

Molly made a canned pineapple upside down cake with a Bisquick crust for her birthday. Nothing to drink to celebrate.

### September 6, 1968

Weather: The weather has been much better this year as compared to last. The past 10 days or so have been especially nice with wind about every direction except southeast. [Southeast winds usually bring wind and rain off Shelikof Strait.] The days are getting cooler and the grass is beginning to turn brown.

Salmon: The salmon are dead and dying. Bill and Joe, two Egegik residents who came up to the lake to go hunting and fishing, caught silver salmon in the lake. They were still good to eat. Most of the reds are so rotten the bears don't seem to eat them. A few red salmon are spawning about a mile up Cleo. The importance of small rain-filled sloughs to spawning salmon is apparent. The presence of these sloughs depends on August rains. They are easy places for bears to catch salmon.

Bears: The bears are spread out. But to state this as fact is difficult because we are almost out of gas and can only walk to Cleo Creek. The lack of bear tracks at creek mouths point out the bears do not use the beaches like they did earlier.

Howie took off to film swans. Molly and I went up on the hill behind Jake's Cabin where we saw the mother with three cubs of yesterday. They were in the same place eating berries. The cubs wrestled, with the light one—the smallest—usually getting the worst of the deal. The two dark ones lead the mother as they moved from place to place and were still fifty yards ahead of her when they moved down onto Cleo. Lead meaning fifty yards.

September 13, 1968

We finally left the lake. The remaining time had been taken up trying to record birds and bears for Howie's film. We were not very successful. Tempers grew short during this period. We spent two days at Norwegian Home with Egegik residents Augie Alto and Bob Meyers and a few other people. There was a big storm during this time making travel off the lake impossible. Spent nights in Augie's gillnetter, as the cabin was full. We went down the lake and rapids in very rough weather, spent the night in a vacant cabin, and continued down the river the next day. We soon ran out of gas and had to beach the skiff and walk for 3 hours to Jesse's cabin. Jesse's husband gave us a tow the rest of the way to Egegik. In Egegik we were treated royally. Hot soup and sandwiches upon arrival at Albrights. Over the years Don Albright had loaned us boats and motors. Steam baths and a moose roast at May Alto's. Flew out on 16th to King Salmon and then on to Anchorage and Fairbanks.

# 10

## How Do You Know That?

Let us not have puny thoughts. Let us think on a greater scale.
Let us not have those of the future decry
our smallness of concept and lack of foresight.

—Adolph Murie

During that winter in Fairbanks, I organized my data, skied, and worked as a carpenter. In the spring, at the suggestion of a family friend, I sent my thesis to Dr. Allen W. Stokes, a professor of wildlife management at Utah State University. He liked what he saw and I was soon accepted into graduate school. Together we started a research project on brown bear social behavior and communication.

I was a little starstruck when I finally came face to face with Allen. I soon realized he knew more about the behavior of birds and mammals than anyone I had ever met, and he was very interested in sharing what he knew. After Allen received chemistry degrees from both Haverford College and Harvard, he pursued a PhD in wildlife management at the University of Wisconsin. His professor was none other than Aldo Leopold, the principal architect of wildlife ecology. As well as being a great teacher and ethologist, Allen was a founder of the Animal Behavior Society. He was one of the first scientists to show the impact of animal behavior on wildlife management plans.

Aldo Leopold had a great influence on Allen's work, as he did and still does on many people, including me. Allen met his wife, Alice, who was Leopold's secretary, at Wisconsin. She worked on preparing many of the essays that appear in *A Sand County Almanac*, Leopold's famous book and the true bible of modern wildlife management.

None of my teachers at Goddard knew about bears or animal

behavior, but they guided me through independent studies and encouraged me to explore on my own by reading and later writing papers. With Allen, however, I got the word directly from the source.

Allen's ecological and behavioral studies of ring-necked pheasants on Pelee Island in Lake Ontario were classic wildlife investigations. His famous Uinta ground squirrel behavioral studies gave me new insights into data collection, ritualized behavior, visual communication as well as observation techniques. A paper Allen and I eventually wrote together about bear behavior and communication is still cited to this day.

Thanks to him I learned to ask—and even sometimes answer—the eternal scientific question, "How do you know that?"

But what Allen taught me best was how to be scientifically objective, an invaluable lesson I have never forgotten. You could never say, "The bear looked at me" when you were with Allen Stokes. You said, "The bear faced me." You can tell which way a bear is *facing*, but you have no justification to say it was *looking*. To prove a bear is looking at you takes experimentation. You have to first develop criteria that allows you to measure, then collect your measurements, analyze the data, and hope it holds up statistically. This became the way I thought and the way I saw.

One day in Utah, Allen took our wildlife class to a local pond to view waterfowl and gulls. He set up spotting scopes and asked each student to identify the different ducks in view. When it was my turn, I had no trouble naming mallard, pintail, teal, and widgeon. Hoping to impress Allen, I noted there were many seagulls around. When I said "seagull," Allen exploded and lectured me on gull identification, emphasizing that what I was seeing were *California* gulls, which just happened to be the state bird of Utah. The word "seagull" has never again passed my lips.

In the fall of 1970, Allen suggested that Molly and I go up to Moose, Wyoming, to visit his friends Adolph and Louise Murie. We knew who the Muries were and were very excited to have the chance to meet them.

Anyone who has ever been active in the preservation and understanding of the planet has had their life touched by Adolph, his brother Olaus, or sister-in-law Margaret Murie, who received the

Presidential Medal of Freedom. Wildlife studies, books, awards, the creation of Arctic National Wildlife Refuge, the Wilderness Act . . . the list of their contributions is pages long. They accomplished great things during their lifetimes, and their gifts of ideas and ethics continue to benefit us all and are testaments to their genius.

Going to Moose to visit the Muries was exciting to say the least. I got to meet the man who had written *The Wolves of Mt. McKinley*, which revolutionized how we think about predatory animals, and who had studied bears for twenty-five summers in Mt. McKinley (now Denali) National Park.

Now in their early seventies, Adolph and Louise made us welcome in their log home on the Snake River. Adolph was interested in what I had done at Lake Becharof and in my plans for the future. He, Molly, and I didn't talk about marking bears, acceptable harvest levels, bear attacks, or the new field of computerized population modeling. Interesting as these subjects were, we all preferred stories about bears being bears, their individuality, and how they moved through their lives.

I showed the couple a film I'd made with some of Howie's footage. They were complimentary. When we got to the section about bears having different faces and different personalities—with portraits of six or seven bears that had come close enough to peer right into Howie's camera—I surreptitiously eyed Adolph as he watched and thought I saw him nod in agreement.

Did he approve of my ideas about individuality? I'll never know. My presumptuous recollection is that he, like me, had no desire to roll up all the bears he had known into one single bear and say, "This is what bears are and this is what they do."

We went back to Moose several times while I was a student at USU and stayed in their small guest cabin next to the Snake River. I will never forget these weekends. The Tetons were beautiful and the Muries gracious. I don't think we ever stopped talking about bears except when we quietly watched a pine marten on their back porch or went across the road to meet Margaret Murie. Not only were the Muries wonderful people, but because of Adolph's knowledge and advice I was able to validate what I learned at Becharof and to plan new inquiries for the future.

I believe 1970 was the last year Louise and Adolph visited Alaska. Adolph died in 1974 and I never had the opportunity to be in Denali when they were. But in 1971 I got a grant and permission from the National Park Service to spend two weeks in the park viewing the same landscapes and bears as they had.

I still have copies of his books on my desk. Every so often I reread a chapter. As well as being a great scientist, Adolph was a fine writer. I pride myself that like him, my observations and conclusions were based on my ability to tell bears apart and see them repeatedly.

So, although our visits were short, Molly and I learned from Adolph Murie. We went from being completely self-taught to learning from another person who had actually sat on the tundra and watched bears. A few words of wisdom from someone you respect goes a very long way.

I didn't go back to Becharof again until 1973. Thanks to Jimmy Carter, Jay Hammond, and other dedicated people, Becharof Lake and much of the surrounding area would become the Becharof National Wildlife Refuge in 1980. The lands encompassing Cleo Creek received special status and became federally designated wilderness, subject to the regulations of the Wilderness Act. Sometimes good things happen.

# THREE

## MCNEIL RIVER

# 11

## Big Rock Candy Mountain

The spring of 1970 found Molly and me about 150 miles northeast of Lake Becharof on Lower Cook Inlet at the McNeil River State Game Sanctuary. We had spent the winter taking classes and working at Utah State in Logan, where I was fortunate enough to receive a small stipend.

After a lot of thought, I decided to do research at McNeil instead of returning to the bears of Becharof. McNeil had one of the world's largest seasonal concentrations of brown bears and the immediate area around it was closed to hunting. I was certain I could observe far more bears here than at Becharof. I was counting on the fact that the dense concentration of bears would allow me to gather information on social behavior more quickly than I could at Becharof. I also hoped to compare the behavior of bears at both places.

At just 128,000 acres or 200 square miles, the McNeil Sanctuary is not large enough to contain the home ranges of all the bears coming to fish in the summer. However, likely because of protection from hunting in nearby Katmai National Park, there were many older bears in the area. This was unlike Becharof, just 150 miles to the south, where hunting was allowed and big males and elderly females were few and far between.

Like the Havasupai Indian who was asked to describe the Grand Canyon and who replied by saying he was the Grand Canyon, brown bears are the McNeil River. Along with the salmon, tides, alders, whales, and glaciers, the bears were my guides to this place.

I couldn't wait for summer to begin. I was so excited to get back into the field after a winter of work.

Then a few days before we planned to fly out, on May 9, my mother called and told me my father had died in a plane crash. We flew from

Fairbanks to Pennsylvania to help with what needed to be done. The giant who had always been there was suddenly missing and my bear studies seemed unimportant and self-indulgent. In spite of the encouragement of many of my father's friends to continue my research, it still took more than a month for me to decide to go back to Alaska.

. . .

On a sunny June morning, Molly and I boarded an Alaska Department of Fish and Game (ADF&G) Grumman "Goose" aircraft in Anchorage. I know it was sunny, as we had waited five days for good flying weather. We flew south down the Kenai Peninsula to the town of Kenai, then southwest across Cook Inlet. We passed Augustine Volcano and began our descent into Kamishak Bay and McNeil Cove. As the plane banked I caught a glimpse of McNeil River and the extraordinary number of bear trails below me, all headed to—or beginning at—the two hundred yards of white water that made up the McNeil River Falls.

A "Goose" is amphibious and can land in the water, put down its wheels, and taxi onto the shore. We landed, drove up onto the beach, unpacked five hundred pounds of food and assorted supplies, and waved as the pilot took off.

If I have a favorite moment in my life it's standing on a beach with Molly watching the plane that has brought us disappear into the sky. We are alone in a new place. For a moment, there is a great enveloping silence. Then suddenly we begin to hear the individual sounds making up where we are. Wind whooshes in the alders, waves slap on the beach, golden crown sparrows sing their plaintive song of three descending clear whistles, savannah sparrows make their buzzing calls, and the ever-present glaucous gulls screech and scream.

It's times like this you can hear the sound of one hand clapping.

This arrival at McNeil was far different than white-knuckling through the white water of the Egegik River rapids and coming out onto Lake Becharof. And I was different, too. Then I was a cowboy, beholden to no one; now I was a married man—Molly and I had gotten married the previous spring—and I also had a responsibility to Allen and the organizations that had given me money.

Most of all I had made a commitment, after the death of my father, that what I was doing was more worthwhile than anything I could have hoped to accomplish in Pennsylvania. Regardless, I was turning my back on a place and people I loved for a life consumed with the behavior of bears.

The land was still brown as green up comes late to Kamishak Bay. There were deep snowdrifts on the beach and hillsides, and no bears in sight. We shoveled through a three-foot snow berm at the top of the beach and post-holed to a small cabin that was to become home for two summers.

For many people, McNeil River is more than a bear sanctuary; it is a state of mind. They consider it the Big Rock Candy Mountain, "a land that's fair and bright," a place where the bears come first and are friendly to humans, where salmon are abundant, and where bears are forever protected from hunting and peacefully die of old age.

I wish this were true.

I knew when I went to McNeil that it was an Alaska State Game Sanctuary and by statute was closed to hunting. This meant hunting could only occur through an act of the state legislature and the signature of the governor, not be "opened" or allowed at the whim of the State Board of Game, a political, pro-predator-control group that establishes hunting seasons and bag limits throughout Alaska favoring increasing numbers of moose and caribou by eliminating wolves and bears.

During July and August the falls on the McNeil famously attract what is thought to be the densest concentration of bears in the world. It is an amazing sight.

It's unlikely, though, that all the summer fishing bears spend their entire lives here or even spend every season of the year here. The McNeil watershed simply doesn't contain enough food for all the bears that visit for the short duration of the chum salmon run. There is no doubt, sadly validated by bears that were marked at McNeil in the late '60s and early '70s—meaning they were tranquilized, collared, tattooed, and given numbered ear tags—that some McNeil bears are killed outside the sanctuary each year in "the harvest," as wildlife managers and hunters like to call it. Hunting is almost certainly the major cause of mortality for the bears that visit McNeil during July and August. Few die of old age.

When brown bears are killed in Alaska, the hunter takes the hide and skull to a Fish and Game office and has both "sealed" and recorded with a numbered metal tag. Large plastic totes work well here. Like a ship in a bottle, it's a bear in a tote—an unnerving and gruesome sight. The length and width of the skull is measured and a tooth extracted for the purpose of aging the bear. A cross section of a bear's tooth looks like the rings of a tree—basically one ring for each year the bear has lived. The hunter is also asked to fill out a form, which asks for the location of the kill.

Examination of these records for areas close to McNeil shows quite a few dead bears, some in their twenties, some as young as three or four, and every once in a while some brave soul bags a two-year-old cub. All lives cut short as bears have been known to live well into their thirties. Shooting any bear is ethically questionable and is far beyond anything I can imagine; however, shooting a bear that has fed next to people every year of its life, like those that visit McNeil River, is quite simply deplorable. Bear hunting is far from a noble pursuit.

McNeil has shown what people can do to preserve a natural phenomenon—in this case, the massing of bears that have come to fish the chum salmon run at the McNeil Falls. However, the fame and mythology of this place have done a disservice to bears in other areas because McNeil exists in a vacuum. The current management theory is "We're protecting bears in one place, so it's okay to shoot them in another."

In 1991 the McNeil River Refuge was created to the north of the McNeil River Sanctuary. Unlike the McNeil Sanctuary, the area wasn't permanently closed to bear hunting. The idea was to place added protection on habitat, in this case a salmon stream. When different groups met to establish the new refuge, professional hunting guides lobbied to have the boundaries placed as close to the sanctuary as possible—all the better to kill protected bears when they moved out of the protected area. They got their way.

When it comes to McNeil, state managers tend to take credit for something they are not responsible for—the fact that bears readily habituate to people and each other where food is plentiful, in this case the salmon-rich McNeil River and the falls that concentrate the migrating fish. ADF&G claims McNeil is the way it is thanks to proper administration, the visitor program, control of the visitor program, and so on.

I've always thought bears call the shots and tolerate humans at feeding sites.

Sadly, as the bear-viewing industry has boomed and there is both interest and economic value in establishing more protected state-run bear-viewing areas, ADF&G has shown little interest. The agency's focus has remained on hunting, the professional guide industry, and maintaining maximum annual harvests.

. . .

In California, one might become a connoisseur of wines; in Alaska, you become a connoisseur of landscapes.

The edge of the North American continent as it erodes into the sea along Kamishak Bay is as spectacular as any shoreline I've seen anywhere in the world. Even without bears, which you frequently see walking the beaches, each turn in the cliffs, tidal meadow, and rock buttress is a thing of beauty and another world to explore. To the south of where the McNeil flows into the sea is McNeil Head, a monolith towering high above the surrounding cliffs. A rock feature a half mile at the base and soaring almost five hundred feet, with only a single ledge—home to a colony of double-crested cormorants—breaks an expanse of conglomerate interspaced with bands of granite and sandstone. It's all evidence of past glaciers, volcanic activity, and massive upheavals as this part of the continent was formed.

Acres of driftwood pushed by wind and tide into huge piles cover parts of the beaches and headlands—Sitka spruce and hemlock from Kodiak, the Kenai Peninsula, and northern Gulf of Alaska; yellow and red cedar from the forests of the southeast part of the state. Occasionally a massive old growth log washes up. These giants become landmarks, before rotting away or floating off in storm surges caused by winter hurricanes. Even without bears Kamishak Bay is an unforgettable place.

Every year I've been there, the landscape looks different. The famous Kamishak weather is the force that dictates what the changes will be. The predominant summer wind, like Lake Becharof, is from the southeast, which brings clouds and rain from the Gulf of Alaska. Most lows in this part of the state track across the gulf and as they pass near McNeil spin off high winds and dump moisture sucked up out of the ocean. A forty-knot summer wind is not uncommon. While westerlies from the Bering Sea blowing across the Alaska Peninsula generally bring fair skies, they, too, can be brutal. Hurricane force winds blow both ways in the winter. A typical National Weather Service winter forecast for west of the Barren Islands and Kamishak Bay waters might be storm warnings with seas to twenty-five feet and northwest winds gusting to seventy knots.

My son captains a boat through these waters as he navigates between Homer and the Bering Sea, traveling "out west" as we say here in Homer, to fish for king crab. Not one to worry his parents, wife, and children about hurricanes and giant waves, he seldom tells us about bad storms, but we know they occur. I think it's curious that he took off for the dangers of the North Pacific and independence of fishing and I left for the Alaska Peninsula to follow brown bears at a similar age.

McNeil Cove is perfectly oriented to receive the brunt of what a southeast wind and accompanying waves can deliver. Because of pounding surf from southeast storms, the sea bottom is hard packed and largely devoid of vegetation, mussels, barnacles, and clams when compared to other nearby coves that are protected by barrier islands. It's a rugged, wild place.

One spring we arrived at McNeil to find the two heavily constructed outhouses blown off their foundations—one went east and one went west—sometime in the preceding winter, storms had blown in from both directions.

Alder-covered hills dotted with open grassy spots stretch behind McNeil Cove. The hills eventually give way to the Aleutian Mountains rising here less than four thousand feet, except for the not too distant Mount Iliamna, which tops ten thousand. It's easy to see that many of these mountains were once active volcanoes, as some have perfect cone shapes on one side while the other is completely missing, destroyed by volcanic explosions and pyroclastic flows.

The tides at McNeil Cove and Kamishak Bay have height of tide differences over twenty-five feet. Several times each month high tides rise over twenty feet ("a twenty-footer" as Alaskans call them) before dropping up to five feet below mean low tide ("a minus five") leaving miles of tidal flats exposed.

McNeil Spit, which extends almost all the way across the back of McNeil Cove, protects hundreds of acres of tidal lands, which in turn produce a rich sedge (*Carex* spp.) meadow. As the sedge ripens the meadow attracts bears. And until it becomes "rank"—as farmers like to say—and loses its high protein levels, there are almost always feeding bears. Ten or fifteen at once is not uncommon in June. Oddly, plantain (*Plantago major*) or goose tongue is not as plentiful at McNeil as it is up and down the coast. This plant, also extremely high in protein, is another sought-after bear food.

At the high-tide line, a sandy area that is only flooded a few times a month, grows a hearty plant commonly called beach greens (*Honckenya peploides*) or scurvy grass. I have yet to see a brown bear grazing on this abundant plant although others have reported it. Beach greens taste just fine before flowering and becoming bitter. Mariners allegedly ate the plant for its high levels of ascorbic acid or vitamin C.

Beach wild rye (*Elymus mollis*), a grass that reaches heights of four or five feet, also grows on these sandy beach berms. It is not a preferred food of brown bears, at least not in Kamishak Bay. It is odd to see a bear eating it despite it being an abundant plant.

Once when I spent a few weeks on a film project in Kukak Bay, about seventy miles south of McNeil, we watched a young bear regularly eating beach wild rye, biting the tops off the stalks, chewing them for a few moments, then spitting out what looked like a cow's cud, in this case not regurgitated but simply well masticated. Why this bear was doing this when literally dozens of others walked by the same plants I do not know. Friends, however, have reported seeing bears, particularly black bears, eating the seed heads off the plant and also eating beach greens. Likewise, some bears will eat the heads off pushki or wild celery plants (*Heracleum maximum*), literally sitting down and dining for extended periods while others will walk through the same stands and keep right on going. Maybe it's the moment or maybe it's the bear—or maybe it's all about nutrition. Perhaps there isn't much fat to be gained from these plants.

Past the top of the beaches the vegetation changes. Up here you see the dramatic effect of the powerful southeast winds. In protected places alder and willow may grow ten feet, but when exposed to the wind, the same plants don't even reach a foot tall, instead growing outward to form green mats as large as one hundred square feet. Tundra patches with caribou lichens and blueberries (*Vaccinium alaskaense*) and crowberries (*Empetrum nigrum*), because of growing close to ground, do well here on the headlands of the eastern side of the Alaska Peninsula. Likewise, wind-resistant grasses do well in areas of mixed vegetation.

· · ·

Coastal sedge meadows and tidal estuaries are critical habitats for brown bears. No two places are the same or grow the exact same vegetation, but barrier islands, sand spits, wind, soil deposits from rivers and streams, and nutrients from the sea all contribute to creating feeding places for bears. Based on the number of bears seen here and the acres of available food, McNeil Cove is certainly one of the most visited intertidal sedge meadows on the hundred miles of shoreline between Bruin Bay to the north and Kaflia Bay on Shelikof Strait to the south.

The biggest and most aggressive bears get the best fishing spots on salmon streams. The same is true of the best vegetation areas. In the back of Kukak Bay in Katmai National Park, seventy-five miles south of McNeil, there is a tidal meadow with different sizes and varieties of sedge. The tallest and greenest grows in the very back, an area covered by the tides less frequently than in front of the estuary. In early June I'd almost always find a few giant bears back there feeding at respectable distances from one another, while subadults, mothers, and cubs kept away. The big males would feed for a while then move off and bed down in the nearby alders, which marked the edge of the tidal influence. I'd see smaller bears out toward the mouth of the estuary where vegetation wasn't so lush.

Bears mate in these coastal meadows during May and throughout June. The fact that mating bears are seen so often here begs these questions: Are these open areas important for bears? Does the fact females come here to feed attract the males that are seeking them out? Mating bears are common at McNeil but many big males don't show up at McNeil until July and the chum salmon run at McNeil River. One would assume these bears mated elsewhere. My many years of observations have shown all the tidal areas of the Kamishak, Ephraim, and Swikshak Rivers, as well as the other numerous bays on the west side of Cook Inlet and Shelikof Strait, are full of mating bears during the spring.

Seasons at McNeil are short. In early June red or sockeye salmon begin to enter the McNeil estuary and mill in the intertidal zone of Mikfik Creek, a short stream that drains Mikfik Lake about three miles inland. As the run builds, swirling salmon attract bears. The Mikfik red salmon run is the earliest salmon run in Lower Cook Inlet and the first fish available for bears.

No one really knows the importance of the McNeil chum salmon to bears. Do some bears suffer because they don't get enough fish at McNeil? What is the importance of other fish runs up and down the coast and over the mountains to the west?

• • •

There are far more unknowns about the McNeil River bears than knowns. For the past forty-five years, the state has steadfastly resisted efforts to do any real research of McNeil bears, so these questions remain unanswered.

When one sees the number of fish present in Bristol Bay streams twenty miles to the west of McNeil and the extensive bear trails leading to them through the Aleutian Range, it's easy to make a guess at least some bears are fishing both sides of the mountains.

Commercial fishing was long thought to be the culprit for the present low fish runs at McNeil, never predation by bears. I've watched McNeil bears literally stop or "cork off" schools of salmon as they make their way upstream. Corks are the floats on top of long drift gill nets, and "cork off" is the term salmon fishermen use when putting a net between a competitor and a moving school of fish, thus preventing the fish from moving into a rival's net and directing them into their own. Fishermen who do this intentionally tend to not have many friends or admirers.

McNeil bears are smart and do the same thing, corking off the few places the fish can navigate through the falls and catching the vast majority as they swim upriver. Fortunately for bear and fish alike, there is enough spawning habitat below the falls to propagate the chum salmon run. The long-term biological effect of this fish catching is unknown; fish and bear numbers seem to ebb and flow with the passing of time. I know of no examples when bears have been the culprits of expurgating a complete salmon run.

I've spent a total of twelve summers at McNeil and visited for short periods several other years. I was there with Molly in 1970 and 1971, then again as an employee of the Alaska Department of Fish and Game from 1990 to 2000. I've had the opportunity to see the age and sex composition of McNeil bears change and watched big and small salmon runs.

I've also seen Fish and Game employee behavior toward bears change over the years. On my last visit there was still a vestigial "the bears may get you" atmosphere and staff carried new automatic shotguns, but it seemed the bears were finally getting through to the humans.

When I first worked for ADF&G, if a bear was slow to leave the McNeil campground it would be progressively hazed out with shouts, cracker shells—large firecrackers fired from a shotgun—as well as rubber bullets, which can be lethal to both humans and bears. Now, hand clapping and stern words are known to be effective, keeping errant bears moving along, away from tents and buildings.

As an ADF&G employee I was required to carry a firearm. When I left McNeil I no longer felt the need. Today I try my best not to have any interchanges with bears except to tell them I'm coming when I'm in a place where I can't see them. I use electric fences while camping to keep them out of my tent, use bear-proof containers to keep them out of my food, and only watch them where I can sit in the open. I try as hard as I can never to stop as I walk, except in places where a bear would have ample opportunity to look me over.

I can remember years ago at McNeil, for no good reason staff would pick up their shotguns—even sometimes placing a shell in the chamber—when a mother and spring cubs came close or two big males decided to duke it out nearby.

Somewhere along the way I started treating bears as bears. This is a big deal when it happens and marks a breakthrough for an observer.

For instance, it doesn't take long to realize a mother can act defensively and protect her cubs, but it is way more difficult to realize she may be bringing her cubs near you because there are no sometimes-predatory males close to where you are sitting. Or to realize the subadult that runs at and by you is doing so not because it's being aggressive, but rather because it's being chased by an intolerant five-hundred-pound female, the small bear not wishing to be bitten on the butt. Bite marks appear on the butts of quite a few young bears.

# 12

## Sex, Drugs, and Confrontation

I n the summer of 1971, there were only a few visitors to McNeil—as compared to hundreds in a season today. The only abodes were two ramshackle cabins, long since replaced with extensive visitor facilities and housing for staff. Fish and Game only visited for short periods, unlike their summer-long presence today. The thirty-year career of sanctuary manager Larry Aumiller hadn't yet begun. Occasionally, friends from Homer would pull their commercial fishing boat into the protection of the McNeil Spit for the night, and we'd walk from the cabins along the shore and go aboard for card games and beer.

When Molly and I arrived in late May, vegetation was still brown, snowdrifts dotted the beach, and we saw very few bears. Early June brought green up with ripening sedges and the gradual appearance of more and more bears.

I set up my spotting scope on the edge of the three-hundred-acre sedge flat and began to record what I saw. In the beginning, I noted only one or two bears a day, but the number grew until there were sometimes fifteen or more bears in sight at one time. Because my main interest was social interactions and how bears went about communicating their intentions to one another, I watched for examples of dominance, subordinance, and play behavior, and took copious notes on interactions between big males and receptive females.

It took about three days of watching bears follow, cavort, and eventually mate to realize much of what had been written about mating behavior came from people's imaginations, not actual observations. For instance, I did not see much evidence of couples staying together for days and weeks as many books had reported.

My observations led me to believe both males and females were promiscuous and mated with multiple partners. There are extremes. Once in a bay about forty miles west of McNeil, I saw the same female and male together for at least ten days. They were the only mature bears in a very small area. Another time I saw a single mature female mate with four different large males in a little over two hours. None of the males fought and the female never moved from an area of roughly four hundred square feet. I know because when the bears left, I went and measured.

Years later I was leading a group of visitors up Mikfik Creek to watch bears at a place called the Upper Falls, a spot on the creek that slowed the passage of salmon and made them easy for bears to grab. On the bottom portion of the creek, we'd watched a female named Teddy mating with a really ugly bear named Earl. We'd all remarked on the multiple scars and open lacerations that had rendered one side of his face mostly scar tissue. Add, or subtract, a missing ear and you have Earl, not a pretty bear but rather the stuff of nightmares. On the other hand, Teddy was one of the best-looking bears at McNeil.

We watched and timed the coupling—thirty-eight minutes my notes read—from about a hundred feet away, keeping up our voyeuristic behavior until the bears separated and slowly walked away up stream, disappearing as the trail passed through high willows. I waited for a respectable time to let them get to wherever they were going, and continued with my group up the same trail the bears had used. There are a several blind corners on this trail and as I came around the last one, about twenty feet in front of me were two bear heads, one on top of the other, both looking at me.

Teddy and Earl were going at it again—and in the middle of the trail, no less. Just as quickly as I saw them, they evidently saw me. They stopped doing what they were doing, separated, turned, and calmly continued up the trail. Was Teddy humming John Lennon's song? "Why don't we do it in the road? Why don't we do it in the road? No one will be watching us."

But I did occasionally see big males fight over females. Seeing one huge animal tear into another is frightening, but altercations are not all that common. Most bears knew their place in the hierarchy, and limiting damaging fights is one of the primary purposes of a hierarchy. On occasion, I have seen two bears fighting with an estrus female nearby. If a third, less dominant male approaches, she is likely to move off with the new bear following, leaving the two original suitors duking it out.

• • •

I spent much of my time at McNeil doing identifications, as only a few of the bears were marked with numbered ear tags before Molly and I got there. I'd look for visible scars and note sex as well as coat, claw, and ear tuff color. The tuffs of a bear's ears can be conspicuous and lighter than the rest of the bear. Bear claws are multicolored, ranging from snow white to deep-dark brown. Sometimes a claw or a canine is missing or broken. This makes them easy to differentiate from one another.

You'd think color would be the easiest way to keep bears straight, but the color of a brown bear gets a bit tricky. Brown bears range from almost white to almost black. In summer their hair is sun-bleached to a shade much lighter than their winter coat. Bears look best when their new, thick coats come in during the fall or when they emerge from their dens in the spring before they've shed. At this time they have solid uniform colors. Lactating females tend to be the last to shed. Males tend to be darker than females. I've seen some light-colored big males but very few dark-colored females. Why I do not know.

At the end of the first week of June, red salmon arrived off the mouth of Mikfik Creek. With the salmon came an increase in the number of mothers, cubs, and subadults. The bears fished the Mikfik red run for a few weeks, concentrating on portions of the creek where the salmon are vulnerable. Toward the end of the month, chum salmon appeared in the white water of the McNeil Falls. Watching bears means learning about salmon behavior too, when they hold in saltwater, when they enter the fresh, and where and when they spawn. As the Mikfik red run slowed, the McNeil chum run increased. More chums meant greater bear numbers each day until the McNeil Falls area contained what is almost certainly the world's largest concentration of brown bears.

The third week of July marked the peak for numbers of salmon and bears. As many as eighty bears have been seen at one time at the

McNeil River Falls. Imagine walking up over that ridge and seeing almost that many feeding together. It is certainly one of the great wildlife spectacles in the world.

During July some bears, particularly mothers with cubs and sub-adults, continued to catch salmon in the bottom portions of Mik-fik. Late July and early August found bear numbers dropping on the McNeil as the chum run dwindled. Curiously, over the mountains to the west, the famous Bristol Bay red salmon run—the world's largest—had entered spawning streams. As the bear numbers dropped at McNeil, they increased on these streams. Bears I've seen at McNeil Cove one day eating salmon have been spotted less than twenty-four hours later twenty-five miles to the west over the Aleutian Mountains feasting on Bristol Bay reds. A few bears stay around at McNeil for the rest of the summer but the majority head elsewhere as other fish runs develop.

When Molly and I got to McNeil, Fish and Game biologists had been doing research on the home ranges and reproductive history of McNeil bears for a number of years. That meant shooting bears with drug-filled darts, immobilizing them, then adorning them with brightly colored collars and ear tags.

McNeil had been a testing ground for drugs, as the staff worked to determine the correct amount needed to anesthetize a bear for a half hour or so. It was a hit-or-miss proposition and, unfortunately, some bears died from overdoses. Several also drowned due to the drugs taking effect as they tried to swim away from the capture crews. A 4 or 5 percent mortality was considered acceptable.

Supposedly, someone at Fish and Game in Anchorage had wanted a reproductive tract from a female brown bear for research purposes. What better place to get it than McNeil River? A technician was dispatched and, legend has it, killed three bears before getting the one he was after.

There were good times at McNeil with more bear activity than I could keep track of, endlessly talking with the visiting Al Stokes, the able help and contributions of our assistant Ron Spry, radio contact should we need help, a good roof to sleep under, resupply flights from time to time, and more red, chum, and silver salmon than we could eat. I even caught a few kings—because of their high fat content, they were the favorite of both us and the bears.

I'd been at McNeil for less than a week and was spending a peaceful evening blissfully sitting alone beneath the bluffs at the edge of the sedge meadow that lies just west of the McNeil Camp. Before me was a big male I named Fred. Fred seemingly kept an eye on me as he walked in circles around an estrus female who was intent on stuffing herself with sedge while managing to remain just out of Fred's reach, moving away every time he got to within a few feet. Abruptly, without any indication of why, Fred turned away from following her and started walking directly toward me. He was a very big bear—think a full-grown Black Angus steer with an outsize head—as large as any bear I'd ever seen. He was also, I was learning, the most dominant bear in the area. His approach made me uneasy. Maybe primordial fear? I honestly don't know. In my four previous years of spending the summers with bears, I'd never had an encounter with a bear this size.

I had little doubt he was focused directly on me. His was not the behavior of a bear just checking me out—cruising by at an oblique angle, keeping a respectable distance of twenty or thirty yards, maybe stopping to sit or lie down. No, Fred strode right in, acting like he was meeting an old friend on the street, ready for a handshake or hug. Because I was sitting, all I could see from my low vantage point was his front legs, enormous chest, his head, and the top of his hump.

For a long moment, it was man and bear—Fred and me—and then an almost involuntary reaction took over. I rose to my feet and very softly said, "Close enough." He immediately stopped, we looked each other in the eye, then he turned and moved slowly away back to the still grazing female.

My note taking had stopped as I was sort of giving Fred my undivided attention, but a few minutes later I wrote in my journal: "No saliva around mouth," a sign of agitation and stress, and "no jaw popping sounds," which are easy to hear at close distances and likely serve the purpose of communicating to other bears—and humans—that more aggressive behavior could be in the offing.

Certainly, Fred was communicating with me, but what exactly was he trying to convey? I have no idea.

I did know I sure didn't want Fred in my face; he was far too big and his teeth looked huge. My bet was he had fetid breath too, just like the bears do in all those bear-attack books available in so many Alaska stores.

Long before I got to McNeil, I'd decided I did not want to touch bears or have bears touch me. Maybe this seems like common sense, but it's pretty easy to have cute, younger bears give you the once-over with a wet, black nose. I know foolish people who allowed this. Certainly, the famous Timothy Treadwell did it. (If you don't know who he is, check out Werner Herzog's film *Grizzly Man*.) Touching is not good for either the bear or myself.

# 13

## Signals and Rituals

t's one thing to look at how bears communicate with humans, like the altercation between Fred and me. But the focal point of all my bear investigations—studying, watching, and dreaming—has always been on social behavior and communication between bears. I knew nothing when I began; now, some fifty years later, I can understand at least some, but certainly not all, of what is being conveyed from one bear to another.

I'd seen many social encounters at Becharof, but it was nothing like the numbers occurring at McNeil. This is why I left the wilds there for the regulated confines of the state-run sanctuary. At the McNeil River Falls I saw more encounters in an hour than I had seen at Becharof in an entire day.

The classic ethological method for investigations of animals is to first carefully describe what you see. I did this at Becharof and continued at McNeil (thank you, Niko Tinbergen). Al Stokes taught me to narrow down my scattered approach to data collection, ask appropriate questions, and focus on exactly what I wanted to learn. Molly helped immensely by identifying each bear that came to McNeil, keeping track of which bear dominated or retreated from another. My job was to look for aggressive behavior I could identify and describe. I knew from Becharof and confirmed at McNeil that a large part of bear communication was based on threatening displays.

At McNeil, just as we had at Becharof, we sat for hours learning about the lives of bears. As I write this, I have boxes on the floor beside me that contain stacks of yellow "Rite in the Rain" notebooks—the icons of a perpetually damp Alaska biologist. Writing in my journal on a late August evening in 1971, after a day at the McNeil River Falls, I tried to succinctly sum up what I had seen that summer.

I'd make myself these little notes to ponder when I was doing data summations. Today they seem a little profound but I still agree and they illustrate where I was on my ethological journey that day and what I believed:

> Brown bears are large and powerful animals capable of causing injury to one another. And their communication reflects this. Threat displays are alternatives to actual fighting.
>
> Brown bears have evolved communication displays that allow the community of bears to function. The displays are made up of individual signals—behavioral characteristics that can be shown to modify the behavior of another animal in a variety of ways, depending on who is communicating and how the signal is perceived.

The displays the bears were showing each other ranged from subtle to overt. When you watched bears visually conversing, you couldn't forget bears also communicated by touching, vocalizing, and smelling—a visual signal could be combined with a vocalization or a reassuring touch. I could only make educated guesses about olfactory signals, but had no doubt of their great importance.

Many of the visual signals used by bears are similar to those of canids—wolves, dogs, and coyotes. The most common ones are body movements: walking, running, sitting, and lying down. When a bear wants another bear to know it's being subordinate, it simply moves away, sits, or lies down. The bear is saying he does not want to fight for dominance, a fishing spot, or an estrus female. A bear who wants to convey dominance, however, may approach another bear at a walk or run.

While the bear walks or runs, it can add other visual signals: It can hold its head up, in a neutral position level with its shoulders, or lower it close to the ground. Its mouth can be open or shut, upper canines may or may not be visible. A bear may use body orientation, standing broadside to an opponent to communicate. It may circle an adversary making short lunges, as it becomes more aggressive. A bear about to make contact may have its ears somewhat flattened against its head. This may signal the bear's intentions, but also protect the ears from bites. Approaching bears often have their ears cocked forward, possibly listening for clues.

As I sat that summer, I came up with a list of about fifty actions bears might express toward one another and carefully described each one. After I identified these signals, I recorded if and how they were used in social situations. In order to say they had communicative value, I had to show they modified the behavior of another bear. I also took thousands of film and video images, which helped me sort things out.

Here's a heavily edited example from my notes:

Bruno is fishing at the McNeil River Falls, facing toward the river he waits for a salmon to swim by. From the bank behind him Fred appears, stopping for only a minute before descending the bank and coming up behind Bruno. Other than approaching at a run directly toward the back end of Bruno, he gives no indication of anything. When Fred is less than 10 feet away, Bruno abruptly turns, drops his head, and backs out of his fishing spot away from the approaching Fred. Fred stops, faces Bruno with a lowered head, and when Bruno is about 20 feet away moves into the exact same spot Bruno had been fishing in. Bruno in turn moves a few more feet, sits, and eventually lies down. Fred makes no move toward him.

One evening in my ongoing journal I wrote, no doubt feeling frustrated:

The collection of information goes from A: English speaking, ethnologically trained, North American, white guy. To B: Alaska Peninsula brown bear who only speaks brown bearese, with a strong local dialect, and lots of body language. To C: Descriptive written analysis, check sheets, statistics, computer science, rain, poor visibility, and fleeting glimpses. To D: The results, which can naturally be shown through statistical analysis to be part of a very strong, irrefutable scientific argument. Don't forget Mark Twain. "There are three kinds of lies: lies, damn lies, and statistics."

• • •

Another question I worked on: Do bears have ritualized behavior when they communicate? The classic definition for ritualistic displays in animals, and in humans, too, is repetitive physical activity performed in regular order that conveys information.

In order to find the answer to my question I made a list of all the visual signals I had identified. Each time two bears had an interaction, I would check off what signals transpired and their order of occurrence. From this data, I was able to ascertain a predictable order of signals that showed bears indeed had ritualistic behavior that conveyed information. It soon became apparent if competition between bears can be resolved with ritualistic, stress-reducing displays, contact and potentially damaging fighting can be avoided. So much for the unpredictable bear of popular lore.

One day I was watching Majesty, a large male, fishing at the most productive fishing spot at the McNeil River Falls—a spot that is almost the exclusive province of big males. Lordship, another big guy, appeared out of the alders and quickly ran down the steep bank, stopping only a foot or two from the fishing Majesty. Just as the law of physics states that "two objects cannot occupy the same space at the same time," two big males cannot occupy the same fishing spot at once.

Within seconds both bears stood facing each other with lowered heads. In all fairness to Majesty, he didn't really have a chance to keep the spot and the fish that went with it. I'd seen Lordship "trash" him a few weeks before when both were intent on the same female, tearing into him with savage bites, forcing him to back away. Majesty was an older bear who looked to be past his prime. Lordship, on the other hand, was buff—and a top bear in the McNeil hierarchy.

With their heads lowered, both bears began the highly ritualistic display we had termed "cowboy walking" years before at Becharof. This was the same communication the bear had used toward Molly and me that long-ago day at Cleo Creek, when we retreated into Lake Becharof.

Moving in slow motion, both bears circled and became stiff-legged, their hind legs appearing almost locked at the knee. They began to pee and drool and, because of their stiff-leggedness and corresponding small steps, looked like they'd lost control of the back ends of their bodies. Heads dropped close to the ground as they circled and moved laterally to each other, mouths remained open. The noise of the falls on the McNeil kept me from hearing their vocalizations.

As was my practice, I had turned on my stopwatch when Lordship had first appeared. I punched it again when Majesty, finally, began to back away after eighty-four seconds of cowboy walking. Lordship sauntered into the fishing spot and Majesty ambled off downstream.

I've watched big males cowboy walking innumerable times. Sometimes it ends peaceably like this encounter did, other times the most horrendous fights ensue. Increased salivation is likely an indicator of stress in these encounters. Brown bears may be the champion droolers of the animal kingdom, like Saint Bernards on steroids. I've seen saliva appear as delicate froth on a bear's lips, and I've seen big continuous ropes of drool reaching all the way from the bear's mouth to ground. If a bear shakes its head or body, something bears often do after an encounter, they can fling saliva several feet.

But, and this is a conundrum I have never been able to solve, I still cannot say with certainty that what looks stressful to me is stressful to a bear.

Ritualistic behavior is not all cowboy walking. That summer, I observed a female brown bear named Penny walking on a bear trail that took her to within a few yards of Lulu, a similar-sized female, feasting on blueberries just off the path. Lulu stopped eating when Penny approached, raising her head and facing in Penny's direction. Penny walked up and touched Lulu with her nose, Lulu reciprocated; soon both bears were nuzzling each other on the head and neck. What I came to call ritualized greeting behavior lasted for a little over a minute. Then, as quickly as the greeting started, it ended. Lulu walked away down the trail and Penny went back to eating berries.

1. Female threatens young male.

2. Female threatens young male. Ears are back with canines covered.

**3.** Females display, "jaw," and vocalize at each other.

**4.** Females display, "jaw," and vocalize at each other.

5. Two females of similar rank in confrontation over fishing spot.

**6.** Two mature males in confrontation.
Bear on left is deferring to the bear on right.

**7.** Two mature males in confrontation.
Bear on left has deferred to the bear on right.

**8.** Battle scars on old male.

**9.** Solstice with fish and spring cub Clyde.

10. Female brown bear chasing salmon.

11. Female brown bear with cub of the year.

12. Solstice fishing with spring cub Clyde on her back.

13. Cub taking refuge under female.

**14.** Cub riding on mother's back.

**15.** Female with two yearlings resting.

**16.** Female with three yearlings in grass.

17. Female with two-and-a-half-year-old cub.

**18.** Two well-furred subadults.

**19.** Two subadults play.

20. Two young males play.

21. Two young males play.

**22.** Bear with fish.

**23.** Bear with fish.

**24.** Big male on hillside in fog.

**25.** Photographer and bears.

**26.** Photographer and bear.

27. Photographer and bears.

28. Photographer and bear.

# 14

## The Crux of the Biscuit–Extraordinary Bears

I started my studies in 1966 with a truly blank notebook—as I've said, I'd never seen a brown bear. I filled in the empty pages with three years of observations. I had learned a great deal at Becharof, and when Molly and I got to McNeil River, I continued my inquiries for two more years.

I was confident that after the years of watching bears in places where they congregated, like Cleo Creek at Becharof and then the McNeil River Falls, I could say the mutual use of resources was the basis for brown bear social behavior. I still feel this way today.

Sitting in the small cabin in McNeil Cove, I pontificated and wrote to remind myself that the amount and kind of foods available were going to be contributing factors to the behavior I was witnessing. It seems simple but I came up with this not-too-original phrase because the density of bears and the amount of food available was so different at McNeil as compared to Becharof, which had unlimited numbers of fish—more than a million returned to the lake each year—spread out over miles of streams, where they could easily be caught. McNeil had only a limited area, the falls on the river, where the chum salmon were vulnerable, a far higher density of bears—perhaps the highest in the world—and a fish run at best in the thousands.

Another day, in another journal entry, I came up with the wise realization—I was young, idealistic, and didn't yet care what others thought of my great and irrefutable conclusions—bears are capable of extraordinary behavior.

And so it went. One day after another sitting at the McNeil River Falls, I found, with so much going on, it was impossible to record everything. I would take my thermos of coffee and several PB&Js, climb under a rock overhang out of the weather in a comfortable chair I'd made from an old wooden barrel, and sit back and watch the show. Taking turns, we'd try to put in eighteen-hour days on the river making observations, counting fish caught and who caught them, who played with whom, which bear dominated another, and so on.

• • •

The data collected at McNeil added to what I knew from Becharof. Now there was no doubt both Becharof and McNeil brown bears lived in dominance hierarchies with top bears and bottom bears. And after cataloging the demise of thousands of fish and who did the catching, I could also state the higher up in the hierarchy a bear was, the more fish it would likely catch per hour.

Again, like at Becharof, mature males at McNeil were at the very top of the ladder. Within this group there was a hierarchy within a hierarchy. Single females and females with cubs were almost always submissive to the big males, but like them had hierarchies within their groups. Everyone picked on the subadults, two-, three-, and four-year-olds, who were and still are my favorite bears.

You have to like subadults. There were lots of them at McNeil, and in turn lots of interactions with other bears. These young bears are the clowns of the bear community and are constantly in motion, getting into trouble, and generally running around as they learn the facts of life. This is as opposed to watching older bears who can be somewhat laid-back while they fish or eat vegetation.

From recording social encounters by these little bears, I learned early on that there was a distinct advantage to having a surviving sibling or siblings. Recently weaned sibling groups sometimes acted as a unit to move other similar-sized bears from prime feeding sites. While it was almost impossible to say these groups cooperated, they frequently approached adversaries en masse. Single subadults generally gave way when one of these groups approached.

Today these sibling groups stick in my mind. I remember the names of the many I've seen and can still picture them. Light and Dark; Red, White, and Blue; and the BMC (for Big Momma's cubs), all at McNeil. Holy Joe and Henderson at Lake Becharof, and Poncho and Lefty at Tuṭuk Creek. There were others. When I stop watching bears, these are the ones I'll miss the most.

• • •

You watch bears do the same thing over and over, keeping score of who dominates who and say that 98 percent of the time bears did this and 96 percent did that and statistical tests of the variables show this. Then, all of a sudden, a bear does something so totally different your science-based stream of consciousness comes to a screaming halt. You're jolted out of your complicity and you remember bears are more than hairy brown lumps with sharp teeth and claws.

Not to debate what Frank Zappa was saying in the song "Stink-Foot," but my understanding is that his line "the crux of the biscuit" means the heart of the matter. These odd things you see bears do aren't random; they are the "crux of the biscuit." They are the things that draw parameters around what brown bears are. They define the bear.

So, while at McNeil I always kept track of behavior that didn't fit with what I normally saw, with the hope of finding new things to investigate that would help me better understand bears.

Here are some of the things I saw.

I witnessed two bears playing, with the much bigger and presumably older bear laying on his back and letting the smaller subadult bear grab and tug on the loose skin around his neck. A famous bear biologist once doubted I'd seen this—as big males are supposed to eat subadults, which they've been known to do, not play with them.

For a month one summer, a subadult female would periodically follow and sometimes play with a much larger female who was accompanied by and nursing two spring cubs. Likely, the subadult was the female's cub from her previous litter and this may be the reason she was tolerant. Whatever was going on is far from common. Every other female in the area chased this subadult when it ventured too close.

I went fifty years never seeing two females attack a single male bear at the same time, but last year at Tutuk Creek, that's exactly what happened. Both females had yearling cubs and the male wandered too close for their comfort. I wouldn't go so far as to say they cooperated but together they brought him down—knocked him off his feet and piled on top of him, in a frenzy of fierce bites. For several long moments, I thought they'd kill him. Somehow he regained his feet, and with lowered head backed off, looking very beaten and defensive. The two females kept him moving with lunging open-mouthed threats, stopping only when he turned and ran.

Then there was the summer of the big but old-looking and decrepit male bear, literally skin and bones with his ribs clearly visible. He was one emaciated bear and looked like a goner. However, he made the most of what I figured was his time left on earth by eating the left-overs of fish caught by other bears. I never saw him catch a fish, but here is the crux of the biscuit. When another big male would catch and start eating a salmon, the old bear would approach on his belly making low moaning sounds. When he got close to the successful bear, he'd extend one front leg and paw out in front and toward the other bear—while continuing to moan—until he slowly, very slowly, using his claws reached out and then drew the fish away. The other bear, instead of attacking or defending, would let it go and simply lick up the salmon blood or any leftover eggs off the ground and go back to fishing. The old bear would back up a few yards with his prize and chow down. He did this repeatedly for the several weeks I watched him.

Maybe the answer for this strange behavior lies elsewhere. Some-times when a female catches a fish and seems reluctant to let her cubs have any, a cub will do a belly crawl just like the old bear and approach its mother with low crying moans until it gets in close enough to hook away the salmon with an extended paw. The crawl-ing, moaning behavior seems to elicit a response in the mother and she usually gives up the fish to the cub.

Then there was the female that acted like a male. A bear we tran-quilized and marked at McNeil was by far the biggest female I had ever seen. She was almost as tall at the shoulder as a mature male, and by August of every year, she rivaled them for bulk. We called her Fat Mary. She was twenty-six years old, which is getting up there for a bear. Because of her size and behavior, we could always recog-nize her even before she got her numbered ear tags.

One day at the beginning of August, I saw Fat Mary playing with the alpha male of McNeil we had named Patches. It could have been mating behavior, as mating pairs do play; however, most but not all breeding takes place in May and June. Patches and Fat Mary were seen daily from July 1 to August 15 but were never seen actually mating. It could have been she had lost her cubs and was coming back into estrus as sometimes happens, except she hadn't had any cubs with her when she appeared in early June and didn't have any cubs the year after she played with Patches. In fact she had never been seen with cubs in previous years. She was odd in that on many occasions she acted like a male displaying at them and forcing her way into the best fishing spots. I have photographs of her fishing shoulder to shoulder with fully grown males on both sides. This is extremely rare behavior. In essence, she became part of the male hierarchy at McNeil.

One last event that shows how elastic and dynamic bear behavior can be. Of all the interactions I've watched, this was the strangest.

It had rained for four days and McNeil River had flooded and turned into a torrent even a bear couldn't stand up in. Fishing and catching had become impossible. One could sit next to the river and only see an occasional bear walking by.

As the McNeil rose, about a mile away Mikfik Creek, a much smaller stream, began to rise too.

Early that morning at the mouth of Mikfik, a fisheries pilot on a stream survey flight had counted about two thousand red salmon. Due to low water and harassment by bears, these fish, the last of a much larger run, had been holding or waiting, reluctant to enter the creek and proceed the three miles or so to the lake where they would spawn. They had tried, but chasing by hungry bears in the shallows at the stream mouth defeated their efforts.

There are two places on Mikfik Creek that slow migrating salmon. The first is the hundred yards of riffles at the mouth where the shallow water makes the salmon vulnerable, and the red salmon were waiting just below these shallows. The second spot and the best location for a bear to catch fish is below a four-foot waterfall about a mile inland. Here the salmon have to jump the barrier before continuing upstream. The best fishing is when the salmon make unsuccessful attempts, fall back, and land on the rocks below, thus becoming easy prey for waiting bears. Marginal fishing also takes place for salmon in the pool immediately below the waterfall. Many bears know about these spots and seasonally, before the McNeil chum salmon begins, it is one of the best places in Lower Cook Inlet to watch bears.

In our story, high water has shut down fishing on the McNeil and Mikfik is fishless due to salmon holding in the deep water off the mouth. Many of the bears that are still around are eating sedges in the intertidal area of McNeil Cove. Things quickly change as the twice-daily tidal current rolls in, holding back, covering the riffles, and deepening the rain-swollen waters of Mikfik. Perhaps in response to the added depth, the fish leave their deep-water sanctuary and begin to swim up the creek.

Not disturbed by fishing bears or shallow water, the whole school swims upstream until the waterfall brings them to a halt.

From high on a nearby bluff, I'd been watching bears in the sedges and the swirls in the water caused by the schooling fish. When I noticed bears leaving the tidal area and heading upstream, I climbed down and quickly followed, finding a place where I could see the waterfall.

Bears, perhaps drawn by the splashing of so many fish in a small area, immediately begin to arrive. The pool below the waterfall where fish had once been difficult to catch was now crammed with red salmon. There were so many there was barely room for fish to swim and no opportunity to get away. Some salmon, trying to escape the giant predators now in the water with them, were forced out of the water and onto the bank, becoming easy pickings. Those still in the water became victims too. Almost every time I saw a big shaggy head come up, it had to a fish in its mouth.

Then things got really weird.

The famous big male bears of McNeil, who should have been fishing at McNeil Falls, began to turn up in numbers. These bears were a rarity at Mikfik because once the chum run begins at McNeil they apparently preferred the big ripe salmon eggs and fat of the larger fish there to the much smaller Mikfik reds.

Now half of the fifteen bears in the creek were these outsize males. Standing shoulder-to-shoulder and even bumping into one another, social stratification seemed forgotten and the lack of aggression shown was astounding. Single females and subadults fished within feet of thousand-pound males, bears they almost always stayed far away from.

Here for ten or fifteen minutes with unlimited food, peace and tranquility ruled among both big and small bears. Life looked pretty good unless you were a fish. Few if any made it out alive.

# 15

## Higher Education

**M**aking a living as a university-based bear biologist was challenging. For two years I spent my winters going to classes and writing research proposals so I could fund my summertime work.

Allen Stokes and I received a grant from Utah State to make a film about brown bear social behavior and communication at McNeil River. Howie, who was still living at Becharof, joined us for a few weeks and did the filming. With the help of a friend who was a professional film editor, my sister's narration, and another friend's musical score, we made a twenty-minute film, *Social Behavior and Communication in the Alaska Brown Bear*. Allen accepted the film in lieu of a thesis. Many universities bought it to use in wildlife and animal behavior classes. I still show it today in my University of Alaska classes on brown bear behavior and conservation.

I wrote a peer-reviewed paper with Allen covering the same subjects shown in the film. The paper has stood the test of time and is still cited today. I also wrote an article for *Natural History Magazine*, which was well received by readers.

When I attended graduate school and did research at McNeil, I had the support of a number of organizations and groups. My biggest contributor by far was the Boone and Crockett Club. The Boone and Crockett Club promotes "fair chase" hunting and habitat conservation, and you can tell a little bit about the flavor of the organization from its name. Started by Teddy Roosevelt in 1887, the organization has done much to preserve wildlife with a focus on big game animals.

I'm eternally grateful for the financial help Boone and Crockett gave me for two years, but I'm not sure how pertinent organizations are today that still promote bear hunting and keep track of who shot the biggest bear.

In 1887 there were just over 1.5 billion people in the world, versus today's total of 7.7 billion. And certainly there are fewer animals and much less habitat now than 130 years ago. So, it's hard to erase the "mine is bigger than yours" mentality of trophy hunters. Me, I prefer to give my money to Planned Parenthood rather than Boone and Crockett or Safari Club International, another organization that supports habitat protection while promoting shooting sports and record keeping for dead animals.

We used to joke at McNeil about brown bear trophy hunters getting sex and hunting mixed up. They couldn't do one so they did the other.

Shortly after leaving Goddard, I had made a short lecture film from some of Howie's Becharof footage. I was invited to show it at an annual meeting of the Boone and Crockett Club, I guess in return for all the money they'd given me. Maybe I shouldn't have taken the monthly stipend, but Molly and I needed it to live on.

I flew back for the dinner, a black-tie affair in the hall of North American Mammals at the American Museum of Natural History in New York City. The two brown bears that overlooked the proceedings from their glass tomb diorama had been killed about two hundred miles south of Lake Becharof. One of the two big males was immortalized in a standing position, possibly in the same pose he was in when he stood up to see what the hell all that commotion was over there . . . Bam!

I'm not sure what you have to do to gain entry to the Boone and Crockett Club, but I believe it's something like kill three species of North American big game and wait for an elderly member to die. There are never more than a hundred members; however, the general public can become associates and send money. It is a very exclusive club.

I was flown first class from Logan, Utah, to JFK, picked up in a limo, and driven to a hotel. That evening the president of GE came by with his chauffer and we drove together to the museum. In the limo was another club member keen on bagging a tiger in India. To his credit, the president of GE told him it was no longer politically correct to do so. I felt it wise not to mention that my uncle and grand-father had killed half a dozen tigers between them.

With a hundred guys—I missed the women if there were any—an open bar, and dozens of glassy-eyed animals looking on, everyone got pretty drunk. I was the youngest person there and quickly sur-mised that no one was going to pay much attention or remember anything I said. However, cocktail hour was only the beginning.

We soon adjourned to a single ornately set table the length of the long hall, beneath the wild critters. Waiters hovered. I can't remem-ber the exact menu but it could have been something like sand grouse from Africa followed by roast *Ovis poli* sheep from Mongolia and filet of young brown bear from Kodiak, possibly all sprinkled with ground rhino horn.

I do remember there was a fifth of scotch, bourbon, or gin for every person there. That's a hundred bottles on the table. No wine, no beer—just the hard stuff. The drinking continued. I did a fine job of keeping up and by the time dessert ended and they brought out the projec-tor, my film, and the brandy, I was in the swing of things. I showed the film, embellished some shots with a few bear stories and got lots of loud applause. Several people came up to talk with me afterward. Remember, these folks were the crème de la crème of big game hunt-ers. They all asked exactly the same thing: "How did you get so close?"

I'm sure I gave the same answer I give today: "Maybe brown bears aren't the animal you think they are."

You can't write about chimps without mentioning Jane Goodall and you can't write about bears without acknowledging Frank and John Craighead. I will always be in awe of what they accomplished. If there are any humans who deserve the title "Mr. Bear," it should be given jointly to both brothers. The invention of radio transmit-ters for animals, research into tranquilization, and their mantra that brown bears couldn't survive without ecosystem management are all part of their lengthy legacy. Thanks to their science and conserva-tion convictions, brown bears were saved from possible extirpation in the Rocky Mountains of Idaho, Wyoming, and Montana. Start-ing with the Craighead's famous Yellowstone Park studies during the late '50s and continuing up until today, bears have been wearing collars and subjected to continually evolving technology like GPS units, satellite links, implants, and television cameras. They have been drugged, tracked, aged, weighed, and had their blood drawn. We can now tell where a bear is, where it has been, what it has eaten, how fat it is, and so on. In the immortal words of Arlo Guthrie in "Alice's Restaurant," bears are continually being "detected and inspected."

• • •

Immobilizing bears, with accepted drug-caused mortalities, was the thing to do in the early '70s. Without capturing and marking, the Craigheads' work would not have been successful.

While at McNeil I worked with Jim Faro of the Alaska Department of Fish and Game capturing bears and outfitting them with numbered ear tags and wide plastic color-coated collars so that bears could be identified from slow-flying airplanes.

Catching bears was the ultimate hunting experience. The folks at Boone and Crockett would have loved it. Stalking a brown bear by crawling in the sedges and shooting it in the butt with a dart gun at close range was exciting.

Even more fun than the actual shooting was looking for the bear after you'd hit it. Sometimes a tranquilized bear would cross the McNeil River and vanish into the alders. We'd mark where we had seen it disappear and follow. Here's where things could get interesting with perhaps twenty or thirty mature male bears in the immediate area.

There are numerous stories in popular hunting magazines of the fearless hunting guide going into the alders after a client's wounded bear—brave man vs. fearsome beast. There are few tales of horribly injured bears and terrified guides trying to find them. Sometimes we looked for bears in dense cover and found individuals that hadn't been darted before finding our quarry. But nothing ever happened to any of us: no charges, maulings, growls, nothing. Surprised bears generally went crashing off through the alders. I still remember the time I was on a fresh trail, pushing my way through a jungle of alders, looking for matted-down grass and footprints. I glanced a few feet to my right and saw a rather large paw attached to an equally large leg. For a moment, I thought I had my bear, only to have one of the kings of McNeil rise from his nap, look me over, and slowly saunter away in the direction of the river.

I took advantage of what I learned. Knowing the age and identity of the marked bears as I watched their behavior certainly added to my research. However, I would never do it again in spite of the fact that modern drugs kill very few bears.

Today Molly and I remember Flower Child, a small, light gray-colored mother bear. With her white ear tuffs that looked like flowers in her hair, peaceful demeanor, and two small cubs, she was a favorite of everyone. We managed to kill her. Jim and I shot her with a dart, watched where she went down, and walked over only to find her already in convulsions, a reaction to the drugs she had just received. She was dead within minutes, her cubs bawling from the nearby alders.

Needless to say, we were all upset. Molly and I still are. We captured the cubs, stuffed them in our packs so they couldn't bite or scratch, and carried them back to camp where Jim got on the radio to headquarters to see if someone could find a zoo who wanted two small bear cubs. The answer from on high came back. The zoos have more than they need, they'll never survive on their own, so put them down. And so we did. RIP.

I can't remember if she was the last bear we tranquilized, she probably wasn't. At the time, other than being saddened, I had no immediate epiphany about handling bears and putting their lives on the line. However, that winter after many conversations with Molly, I decided the kind of research where bears' lives were at stake, along with the emotional cost, was okay for others but not for me. I simply no longer had the desire to interfere with the lives of bears.

All I wanted to do was watch bears being bears. If handling bears really needed to be done to perpetuate the species, I was happy to leave it to other people. Their results were often fascinating but I'd made my decision. I didn't want to have the kind of relationship with a bear that comes from overpowering it and subjecting it to something it surely didn't want.

I didn't need to collar bears to know they went through the mountain passes between Katmai National Park and McNeil River when the Bristol Bay red salmon run began. I didn't need a tranquilizer gun to know there were few bears at Becharof in May and June, and fewer at McNeil in May and October. For me to see Fossey and her four spring cubs at McNeil one day and less than twenty-four hours later hear that they sat down next to my friend Chris twenty miles away at Wolf Lake in the Katmai Preserve was just as important to me as knowing some marked animals had made similar trips.

Or maybe I never grew up and I'm still riding my horse through the Pennsylvania countryside, interpreting and wondering at the natural world as I ride along, and being a hopeless hedonist who prefers lying in the mosses and lichens of Alaskan tundra to having any responsibilities.

Largely due to photographers, who didn't want collars and ear tags in their photos, marking bears stopped at McNeil in the '70s. Since then staff has been using photographs, age, sex, reproductive condition, size, scars, claw and coat color, facial characteristics, and behavior to identify bears. Everyone who works there is happy with the results, which if nothing else supports their bear stories. Like them, I have no problem with identifying individuals in places I visit—no two bears ever look the same. Occasionally my ability to do these identifications is questioned by members of the scientific community. I like to point out I have absolutely no problem with telling my black Lab from others of his breed.

Perhaps it is time for biologists to ask themselves as they lean out of helicopters and prepare to dart terrified bears, Why am I doing this? Isn't there a better way? After all, the bear already knows who he is, where he lives, and what he likes to eat. Once I sat on a stream bank with a biologist who was in charge of one of Alaska's most imperiled populations of brown bears. During his twenty-five years with the ADF&G, he had "sealed" hundreds of bears and killed I don't know how many more. He didn't like bears.

The fish on this particular creek were making a run for their spawning grounds and some very intent bears were fishing in front of us, some within fifteen or twenty feet.

As the guy clutched his shotgun while watching the bears in obvious awe, he murmured, "This is as close as I've ever been to a bear I wasn't skinning." He said it twice.

Few bear biologists have the time or inclination to spend hours, days, and years simply sitting and watching or perhaps following individual bears over the landscape. Both the state and federal governments have chosen to treat bears as populations and not as individuals.

# 16

## Hell for Stout

**M**olly and I grew to love Alaska and decided to spend the following winter, 1971–72, in Fairbanks. Except for visiting family and taking vacations, we've never left the state. I didn't go back to McNeil the next year. Allen Stokes wanted more students in the bear study, the numbers of visitors at McNeil were dramatically increasing, and I wanted out.

The green hills of Becharof began to look pretty good again. Sitting, cold and wet on Cleo Creek with the wind blowing the rain horizontally, and watching just a few bears had a lot more appeal than being with Fish and Game staff, tourists, and new grad students at McNeil. I couldn't wait to head out by myself in the morning, find a mother and cubs, and see if I could stay with her all day.

In the next few years, several graduate students received degrees from work they did on what came to be known as the Utah State Bear Study. My research appeared in several theses and dissertations without giving me the credit I felt I deserved. Such is life. I was young, naive, and hadn't known academia could be a cutthroat business.

The next logical step would have been a position as a game biologist and bureaucrat with the Alaska Department of Fish and Game. I knew that would be a terrible fit. Instead I worked as a carpenter to support our growing family. My son Ivan was born in Fairbanks in 1972, followed by Otto in 1975.

We had purchased property in Homer in 1974 and moved there permanently in 1975. I had been building log houses in Fairbanks and went at it full-time in Homer. Molly and I and our sons Ivan and Otto built our own house some fifteen miles out of town. We still live there.

I returned to Becharof without Molly in 1972 and then visited with Howie a handful of times in the next few years. Howie's last year at Becharof was 1981.

For the next ten years, it was all about family, making money, and building log houses. I found that working and chasing bears were mutually exclusive.

About the only bears I saw, except for tracks, were the plentiful black bears that live around Kachemak Bay, which I saw sometimes on my way to work or while hunting for our annual moose.

In 1987 I joined my friends Renn Tolman and Mary Griswold on their seven-hundred-mile round trip from Homer to Bristol Bay in a Tolman skiff, which they designed and constructed.

Tolman skiffs are now world-famous boats you can construct yourself. Hundreds of people have built their own following the directions in the book Renn wrote, *Building the Tolman Skiff*. Renn has sadly passed on but his legacy of fast, light, economical boats will endure for generations to come.

The adventures of Renn and Mary would fill a book by themselves, as would their musical, dancing, and skiing accomplishments. While many of us sit at home and imagine trips into the wild, these two did them. Not once but again and again, year after year. They knew the waters and bays of western Cook Inlet, Kamishak Bay, and the Kodiak Islands as well as anyone. They'd spent years exploring cove after cove, anchorage after anchorage, mountain after mountain.

Ask Renn where to anchor up in Bruin Bay and he would say, "You can get in there behind the old weather station and you're good— except if you get a really hard westerly. Don't go in unless you have at least half water and a rising tide. Watch out for rocks on the way in and when you anchor." He wouldn't mention the part where you had to traverse close to eighty miles of open water to get to Bruin Bay from Homer.

Mary is tall, lean, and attractive with tousled brown hair. She frequently wears a baseball cap when she is outside and always has a dog with her. The dog's name is always Kami, named after Kamishak Bay. With her great charm and intellect, I doubt if she has ever not helped a person or organization that needed her. A master carpenter, she constructed houses for years and built and designed the early

Tolman skiffs with Renn. The most praise Renn ever heaped on any builder was "He can do it all." And Mary can do it all.

Once when I stopped by their shop—stopping and talking boats was one of my favorite things to do—Renn was lofting a new skiff. I marveled at his ability to measure.

He said, "I just trig it." From Mary's work station where she was building transoms came a very un-Mary remark, "I taught him trigonometry."

Mary still burns coal, which she collects off Homer beaches for warmth, and shoots a deer to eat on her annual solitary voyage to Kodiak in her boat, the "Pennywhistle." She cans salmon and freezes ducks and halibut. She's an accomplished flutist and never misses a contra dance, where she plays as well as participates.

Not only did Renn build houses and boats but he and Mary put on weekly dances in his boat shop. He played flute and pennywhistle and taught step dancing to anyone interested. Each year he made a trip to Cape Breton to participate in the dances he loved.

Grizzled and rugged looking from a lifetime outdoors, he was otherwise physically nondescript and of ordinary size. He didn't seem a powerhouse until you soon realized while playing tennis he was just being nice and could have trashed you at will. The same for skiing. He'd politely wait for me to catch up and then patiently offer encouragement. Try skiing with a man who had been downhilling since the age of two, started the ski patrol in Aspen, and when on his yearly jaunt to Jackson, Wyoming, had "first tracks" at Jackson's most famous runs.

Renn was a "runner." It's a construction term used to describe the very few who go at it as hard as Renn. He moved quickly when he worked, sometimes breaking into a run as he went for a tool or a board. He never stopped. I asked him once why there were no windows in his shop. He replied, "Having windows is unfair. You don't look out the windows when you work."

Renn was witty and had a wry, Yankee sense of humor. After all, he was from New Hampshire. I never heard of anyone he wouldn't help. About the only people he was critical of were other boat builders.

There are many Renn and Mary stories out there. I include this one because it was one of the best Alaska journeys I have ever been on, but it also took me back to trips with Howie and Molly.

Before I met Renn, Mary, and Kami the dog in Egegik, here's what they had already done: They started this adventure at the Homer harbor, crossed forty miles of Cook Inlet to Iliamna Bay, had the skiff trucked fifteen miles over the mountains to Pile Bay on Lake Iliamna, then motored seventy miles west on the lake—the largest in Alaska—then fifty miles down the Kvichak River to the coast and the Bering Sea and finally south forty miles to Egegik.

Together, we then proceeded up the Egegik River, through the rapids that were by now familiar to me, and down the lake to set up our tents on the very same island Molly, Howie, and I had camped on some fifteen years before.

It rained and the wind blew every single day during the two weeks we spent on the lake. We went out every day no matter what the weather, hiking to places I'd never been and seeing bears, wolves, moose, and dozens of caribou. In those days before habitat changes and over-hunting, Becharof was called the Serengeti of Alaska. There was game everywhere.

On this trip we only saw five or six bears every day. However, the famous Bristol Bay red salmon run was still weeks away and there were no salmon in the lake. With no fish to eat, the bears were widely scattered. The mothers and cubs observed were feeding on vegetation in the uplands. We didn't attempt to follow them, only watching from a distance. My field notes tell of being approached twice by young bears and followed once by two small bears who were traveling together.

June 1, 1986

East End Becharof. Left island at 7 a.m. in hard SE wind. Left skiff at mouth of Bear Creek and hiked directly east toward mountains. Herd of 19 caribou ½ mile away. Stopped for lunch around 11 a.m. on mountainside. Single small bear—feeding?—in tundra about 200 yards away. Slowly moved in our direction. Kept coming to 100 feet. Stopped. Turned. Went OOS [out of sight] downhill to south.

June 5, 1986

East End Becharof. A non-event. Hiking to mouth of Kejulik across
base of Severson Peninsula with Mary. Trying to find Jay Hammond's
second cabin at the outlet. Driving rain. Renn made warming fire in
a small cottonwood grove. Smarter than we were. Noted two small
bears—¼ mile?—behind us. Maybe following and maybe not. We
were on same bear trail. Moved 50 yards uphill off trail. Got out
sandwiches. Bears eventually passed us. Finished eating. Never saw
bears again.

I would never have been able to recognize Holy Joe and Henderson, as familiar as they once were to me. By this time, they would
have been very big bears, looking nothing like they did when they
were cubs. I still had a wonderful time seeing new bears, visiting old
places, and walking familiar trails.

Camping at the mouth of Featherly Creek one night, we built a
fire on the lakeshore beach to warm us up and to cook some trout.
Renn and Mary never used gas stoves. Someone—my guess Crazy
Billy—had torched Norwegian Home, so we couldn't stay there.
Renn wouldn't have slept inside anyway, always preferring his tent.

We soon retired to our tents as the wind was blowing at about
thirty knots. We were in a protected spot but it was still miserable.
Sometime in the night we discovered our sleeping bags were getting wet. As it blew down thirty miles of open water, the wind had
created a seiche, causing the water on the downwind side of the lake
to rise more than a foot. Our nice campsite was swimming, covered
with water, and the shore side campfire had floated away. We later
learned the wind had gusted over one hundred knots in Egegik. On
the Beaufort Wind Scale, wind blowing harder than sixty-four knots
is a hurricane. Lucky for us, we were in a protected spot.

Back in 1966 Molly, Howie, and I had hiked the old Kanatak Portage trail. Used for at least five thousand years, it was the route of
residents and Russians alike as they went from the Bering Sea to
Shelikof Strait and evidently on to Kodiak. The trail goes through
the mountains from Becharof to the old town of Kanatak and Portage Bay on Shelikof Strait.

After I recounted that journey, Renn, Mary, and I decided to retrace the route. We found the trail without difficulty and climbed up through the pass to where we could see Shelikof and the old village site. We looked down on an ocean filled with huge breaking combers and a dozen Kodiak seiners anchored and hiding from high winds in Portage Bay. The wind was blowing hard where we were too. You could stretch out your arms, lean back, and it would almost hold you upright. Enough was enough—we quit our trip about two miles short of salt water.

After two weeks, we were running low on food and we were tiring of a bland and continuous diet of Arctic grayling and Dolly Varden trout. The wind continued to come from the southeast, which meant blowing down the length of the lake, directly into the top of the Egegik River. The river starts and then winds through a series of uniformly low hills that mark the end of the lake. Unless you're right on top of it, the outlet is difficult to see from the elevation of a small skiff. People in Egegik had warned me numerous times not to leave the lake in a southeasterly wind, as breaking waves makes the approach and mouth of the river treacherous. Molly and I had once waited for over a week at Norwegian Home for the wind to slack off and the waves to diminish.

This time Renn, Mary, and I waited four days, and when the thirty-knot winds dropped to between fifteen and twenty we set out. As we motored down the lake, we had following three-foot seas. Tolman skiffs are mighty good sea-going boats and we enjoyed a thrilling ride, surfing down waves for more than thirty miles.

As we approached the river, we were suddenly in the middle of six-to-eight-foot waves with the tops being blown off as all the wind and wave energy of the lake was driven into shallow water. There was nowhere to turn back to and no place to hide. Huge boulders appeared in the troughs between the waves and we were in real danger of being swamped or flipped.

Mary and I were hanging onto the gunnels when a huge rogue wave almost broke on us. I can still picture Renn in the stern as the boat was propelled sideways toward the shallows and disaster. Somehow, he clung to the tiller handle and turned the boat ninety degrees on the actual face—right below the breaking crest—of the massive wave. The boat responded perfectly, the bow stayed up as it was designed to do, and we surfed past the rocks and into the protection of the river.

Renn used to say Tolman skiffs were "hell for stout." This one sure was.

• • •

Howie continued to go back to Becharof until 1981, well after our trips together stopped. Sometimes he spent summers by himself and sometimes he had company. On the short trips I made to visit, he seemed happy enough, and he still didn't mind getting cold, wet, and avoiding creature comforts. I've always wondered if his body finally couldn't keep up with his mind and he ultimately succumbed to the elements as he pursued what he liked to call "the itness of such."

Howie loved bears, was worried about their future, and felt the beauty of his films could help conserve them.

There was no last time watching bears with Howie. Maybe it was a day of trying to put names on the multitude of green colors that make up the Becharof landscape, or guessing the strength of the wind, the number of red salmon, or the size of a brown bear we watched.

Maybe we had ptarmigan for supper with a side of trout or grayling. Maybe we saw sandhill cranes and trumpeter swans as they gathered in the tundra or circled high riding the thermals looking for favorable winds to carry them south. Maybe we sat together on a hillside and watched a mother and cubs eating blueberries. Time has made Becharof days blend together.

I do cherish memories of Howie as I look again at the films I made using his footage. I see the bears through his eyes. This is a rare honor, one I am eternally grateful for.

In the last scene in the movie, I showed to the Boone and Crockett Club, a mother and three yearlings run and play far away from us on a hilltop. Howie captured and framed them as four tiny bears silhouetted against the evening sky.

More frames show the mother and four yearlings we found on the hike to Ugashik Lake. All five bears are lying down facing the camera with the smallest cub touching the mother. In another shot I see a bear called Dinty Moore (after the canned stew we sometimes ate) with his nose to the ground following our tracks to within feet of where we stood filming.

It's impossible for me to watch that footage without thinking of Howie. Howie was a talented cinematographer and his shots were carefully planned. He might want a bear walking into, across, and then out of an image he had framed, or perhaps he'd start his camera on a swimming salmon and pan slowly up to the face of a waiting bear.

Sometimes we'd pretend the bears were on a stage and we were filming them from the perspective of the audience. Howie would get his camera ready, frame the scene he wanted, and keep his eye near the viewfinder of his camera. I'd stay on the lookout for bears that might walk into his planned shot. If one cooperated, I quietly say stage right or stage left, trying to remember—and usually forgetting—if it was the bear's left or right not mine. Howie would stop when I got it wrong and we'd both break into laughter.

Jackie Abluma, the man who first guided Howie and me through the rapids on the Egegik River, told me his uncle and aunt were very likely the last people who ever saw Howie. They'd flown some seventy miles from Egegik in their own plane and landed on the beach in front of the old abandoned village of Kanatak on Shelikof Strait. They found Howie sitting in his sleeping bag, leaning up against the inside wall of the old schoolhouse. He looked sick, but was coherent as he told them a plane was coming in from Kodiak to pick him up the next day.

Worried, they tried to talk him into flying back to Egegik with them. He wouldn't budge, and they left him—along with his Arriflex movie camera, a red Kelty backpack, a little food, dry clothes, and the shelter of the building. That night or the next morning, he disappeared. No one's ever seen him again since that early September 1981.

In his book *Bush Rat Governor*, Jay Hammond wrote: "Of those who've lived among brown bear, no one did so with such intimacy as Howie Bass. Howie had a consuming passion to learn everything about these giant omnivores. . . . I have no doubt his film library included more fine bear footage than exists anywhere."

Unfortunately, Howie's bear film library disappeared along with Howie. We think he discarded it before he made his final trip to the lake. He'd also recut a few earlier films on other subjects, ruining, at least in my opinion, his beautifully crafted work. His only surviving bear footage—what remains of hundreds of hours of his painstaking shooting is what appears in the two films I made.

Jay knew Howie and how relaxed he was around bears. He believes a bear killed him. Crazy Billy Nekeferoff actually vanished around the same time Howie did, although the locals say he drowned in the Egegik River.

Here's the thing: People sometimes disappear in Alaska. It's big country. One day they're there, the next day they're not and the reason is often not clear. I like to think Howie started climbing the mountains between Kanatak and Becharof, wandered off the trail, sat down to rest under some alders, and never got up.

On that trip with Renn and Mary to the places where Howie and I had been so many times, I looked for signs of my friend. In spite of walking the very same trails and camping in the very same spots, I never saw a trace of him.

# FOUR

## INDIVIDUALS AND OPPORTUNISTS

# 17

## Return to McNeil

In 1991, thanks to Larry Aumiller, I was offered a summer job at McNeil River. I had no problem saying yes. I'd been missing the bears, was burnt out building log houses, and truthfully had never thought I'd be spending entire summers in the field again.

I now also owned a furniture shop where I could work in the winter, and Molly had her master's degree and the job she wanted as a clinical social worker. Ivan and Otto, like other industrious Homer kids, had high-paying jobs on commercial fishing boats and were gone most of the summer. Children grow up quickly around here.

So, the kids were "highliners," top fishermen on top boats, and well able to take care of themselves. Molly was the chief breadwinner, making more money than I ever had. I just had to keep my skis waxed, the home fires burning, and build rocking chairs and kitchen cabinets from time to time.

Maybe I'm more like a bear than I think—shut down in the winter—get going when it thaws in the spring. For years I quit working outside when the winter storms moved in and temperatures dropped. Late October and twenty below in Fairbanks is not a good time to drive nails. I remember the time a cohort and I were nailing window trim on a house we were hurriedly finishing in minus zero temperatures. He drove a nail and a piece of wood split off a frozen windowsill, wrecking what was supposed to be a perfect fit. He found the wood chunk on the ground, looked at it for a moment, than spat on it, and stuck it back where it had come from. It instantly froze into place.

Anyway, I've always preferred seasonal work, kicking back in the winter and spending time keeping warm. I completely understand hibernation.

When I returned to McNeil as an employee of the Alaska Department of Fish and Game, my job was to guide tourists to see bears. I did this for three months each summer for the next ten years. I figured it was up to me to keep the bears safe from the people, but naturally the state saw it the other way around. We were required to keep our guns close and well-oiled.

In 1970, when I first visited, anyone could go to McNeil anytime. By 1991 things had changed. The permit system for sanctuary entry greatly limited the number of visitors. Most of the sanctuary was now off-limits to people unless they were accompanied by Fish and Game staff.

By regulation, bear-viewing groups were limited to ten people or fewer. There was no scientific reason neither for this nor for the viewing hours, which almost always occurred between 10 a.m. and 7 p.m. The notion was that not having people at the viewing areas at other hours gave the shy-of-humans bears a chance to come in and feed. This went against what I had seen elsewhere—that at least some of the bears feeding in the less productive fishing times of early morning and late evening were avoiding more dominant bears, not people.

The people trail, on which I lead my groups to the McNeil Falls, starts at tidewater near the mouth of the river. Before it was a people trail, it belonged solely to the bears. After passing through a break in the bluffs that separates the tidal area from the uplands, it parallels but stays away from and out of sight of the river for about a mile before turning and descending downhill through open grasslands.

Coming over the last rise and looking down on the river and suddenly having fifty or sixty bears come into view is unforgettable.

When we got to this spot, I heard things like "Unlike any other!" "I've never seen anything like this!" "I couldn't have imagined." "We've got to protect this place!"

A few cry at the sight. Actually, one woman fell to her knees and thanked the Lord. Not a bad idea. It is a deeply personal and moving experience, one I treasured every day I had the privilege of walking to the falls and coming over that rise.

The McNeil Falls is a hard picture to paint, and it's not a still life. The few bears up or down stream do not draw your attention; it's the ones that are massed in the river and on the banks of a two-hundred-by-one-hundred-yard area. Here the river breaks over a series of rock slabs, the only place where salmon are vulnerable as they pass through shallow water and up over small waterfalls. There are no trees, only dense alders that grow everywhere except on the river-banks. At first the bears are simple brown spots, then they become individuals, then they turn into big males, then single females, then small bears, then mothers with cubs. Next the whole tableau begins to move and what is surely the biggest event in the bear-viewing world begins to unfold.

On top of a level rock outcropping at the river's edge is a man-made gravel "upper pad" where visitors and staff are required to sit. Immediately below and part of the same rock formation is the "lower pad," which provides additional space. Since group size is limited to ten, the idea is sit half up above and half below. Having groups of five and five is also less stressful for the bears that are constantly walking by, often within just a few feet.

If it's sunny, people want to be above, and if it's rainy they want to be below as there is some protection from the rock overhang. Pro-fessional photographers, of whom there are many—McNeil is like a destination resort for them—size up where they want to be the minute they get to the river. The upper pad is where they feel they can get the best shots. Staking out seats can get aggressive.

Midway through the day the people on top go below and vice versa. The occupiers of the primo spot at the end of the upper pad typically had hearing difficulties. I never played favorites and always preferred the plain folks who just wanted to know about bears, regard-less of where they sat.

• • •

One of these folks was Jennifer Wells, who came to McNeil in her twenties and joined a group I was guiding. Now an Alaska Superior Court judge, Jennifer is quite articulate and clearly remembered her visit nearly twenty years earlier.

Without thinking, she applied for a permit to visit McNeil, got one, and almost didn't go. A friend encouraged her, explaining it would be an experience of a lifetime and she shouldn't pass up the chance. So, without knowing much about bears, she went.

I talked with her recently—to see what she remembered and to hear the language she used. She described the experience as "life changing" and I realized she didn't mean it in the sense she had gone from being scared of bears to becoming an advocate—a common reaction for McNeil visitors—but rather she had experienced something powerful and wild by being, as she described it, "allowed into the bear's world."

Jennifer had moved to Alaska from the East Coast with a "craving for wilderness" and at McNeil she got what she wanted.

> It was such a privilege to be there, in a place a person is not supposed to be. The bears made me feel small in comparison to their power and wildness . . . watching them be bears, catching fish, nursing young, hearing the sucking of cubs. I felt I was somewhere private and sacred. From a human perspective, it was very humbling and so powerful at a core gut level. I went from having a one-dimensional sense of bears to something entirely different. I was able to become an observer of their lives.

Jennifer went from knowing nothing of bears and being someone who wanted to experience wilderness and wildness to someone who felt at ease when walking in Alaska. An avid hiker, she's had two bear encounters since her McNeil visits. In the first one she remained calm, did not run, felt very small, stood her ground, and the bear turned and ran. In the other encounter, she and a friend left the trail to the bear and the bear passed on by. She credited her ability to navigate both situations to having visited McNeil.

• • •

On the other side of the world from McNeil, a friend of mine has been taking people on walking safaris in Africa for thirty years. They go out to see, among other things, the Big Five—lions, leopards, rhinos, elephants, and Cape buffalo—which are all on his trip itineraries.

He has the same attitude toward African animals that I do toward bears—and, like me, he has never had any problems with the savage beasts. What he says might sound familiar by now: "Watch the animal and when it tells you it doesn't want you there, move away."

Long ago he stopped taking professional photographers and film crews on trips, knowing they'd be continually pushing both him and the animals. It's the same old story I've seen so much of at McNeil as people come to film and photograph bears. It's no longer about the animals, it's about the shot.

The Alaska Department of Fish and Game and particularly sanctuary manager Larry Aumiller deserve enormous credit for the world-famous visitor program at McNeil. At least two books and innumerable articles have been written about Larry. His thoughts and ideas about bears have become gospel. His determination and perseverance have led to a wonderful visitor program founded on the idea that "the bears come first."

However, after having watched people and bears interact in other places, I believe it is the behavior of the bears as well as the stringent visitor regulations that has made McNeil what it is. Bears habituate to people the same way they habituate to each other. The Alaska Department of Fish and Game has merely taken advantage of what bears do. The bears deserve credit, too.

Larry and I didn't always perceive and understand bears the same way. Over the years I've seen things he hasn't, and I'm sure during his thirty years at McNeil, vice versa. Even when we were observing the same event, like watching two big males have an interaction, Larry and I couldn't always agree on what was going on.

There was no hard science done when I was at McNeil and none was encouraged. Fish and Game rejected efforts by academic researchers because of possible negative effects on the visitor program. This really bothered me. Fish and bears were counted and bears were identified but nothing was added to our knowledge except for what I felt was anecdotal information—and this in a place that is the greatest laboratory in the world to study and learn about free-living brown bears.

Prior to returning to McNeil, I'd been running my own construction company and crews, meeting payrolls, making a profit, and always doing a good job. Working environment, wages, and employee satisfaction were the order of the day. I've always had the philosophy of Randy Newman's song "Have Pity on the Working Man." I wasn't happy with the bureaucracy of Fish and Game and for the most part I felt I didn't fit in. I took me a while to realize McNeil was really someone else's domain, and I was just staff. I did however give it my best shot.

By 1990 the Fish and Game tally for the sanctuary had climbed to more than one hundred bears. There are many reasons for the increases—a reduction of bear "harvest" levels on the Alaska Peninsula, better management of the Bristol Bay red salmon run that ensured a more constant supply of fish, hunting closures in nearby areas, and added protection due to increases in the size of Katmai National Park had doubtlessly been contributing factors. The intertidal pink salmon were about gone as was the small run of kings. In my ten years there, I doubt if I saw more than a dozen king salmon caught by bears.

Except keeping a record of who played with whom, science stopped for me in 1990, although I did continue to keep a descriptive journal of what I saw. Answering questions and keeping people away from the bears was my job. True, each day we identified and counted bears and kept track of how many fish they caught. These numbers and fish counts always seemed a little rough, but I guess they indicated something, exactly what I do not know.

When you look at the data put together by ADF&G, it shows that around one hundred different bears visit the sanctuary each summer with counts of fifty or sixty bears in sight at once at the falls area. These are considered satisfactory numbers by ADF&G. If the bear numbers at McNeil plummeted? ADF&G might do something, but given current management, state statutes, and the agency bureaucracy, I sincerely doubt it. Since at least 1980—and most likely before—the State of Alaska has tried to reduce brown bear numbers through adoption of progressively liberal hunting regulations. A few less bears at McNeil would make some people in Fish and Game and the hunting public very happy.

In the early 1990s staff at McNeil received an official notice from headquarters in Juneau telling us to refrain from naming bears. My guess is that someone, in some twisted way, thought this made bears less desirable trophies, after all would you want to shoot a bear named Sweetie Pie or Snuggles—or Flower Child or Majesty? We were also ordered to stay forty yards away from the bears, which is not possible at McNeil given that the viewing platform at the McNeil Falls was only feet from the river and many bears had habituated to people enough to pass by almost within touching distance.

We all thought it was BS and we didn't pay attention to either new regulation. We may have all gone outside and faced southeast toward Fish and Game headquarters in Juneau and raised our middle fingers. If we didn't, I wish we had.

Most of the game biologists who visited McNeil weren't scared of bears, but some were. One Fish and Game supervisor visited and never took off his shoulder-holstered 44-magnum pistol—even in the campground and when talking to visitors. He was known for his desire to machine-gun wolves from airplanes; he didn't rank high on my list.

When he arrived by plane for a four-day visit, Larry departed on the outgoing flight, leaving me to entertain the guy.

A top Fish and Game administrator came in with his cronies, as the trip to McNeil was a perk of his position. Larry again left me to take care of the bigwig who stayed drunk pretty much all the time and was no threat to the bears. He did tell bear stories, which were all the same: big, dead, record-book bear, and hero-hunter suffering unimaginable hardships before confronting and killing the mighty bruin. I just listened.

What can you say to a person who has had the "McNeil Experience" of wandering around among real live brown bears and still insists—I guess, believes—that bears are bloodthirsty creatures put on the earth for him to kill? I never put much stock in arguing with drunks either.

# 18

## Being Alpha

In 1991 a big dark bear showed up in the sedge flats at the mouth of the McNeil. Ignoring the memo, we called him Woofie for the woofing sounds he made from time to time. He might have been in the area since childhood and adolescence, but as I wasn't there I had no way of knowing. When I first saw him, he was fully grown or very close to it.

If you're wondering how big a "big male" is, there are records of male brown bears weighing fifteen hundred pounds. I would have to assume this is fall weight, after the summer's eating frenzy. Males can gain more than 40 percent of their body weight between spring and fall. This means a bear that weighs in at a thousand pounds in May might tip the scales at fourteen hundred by November. Genetics, hibernation periods, and food supply all effect bear weight. Male bears are difficult to weigh because they are so large and because they are seldom handled by biologists. Plus, it's hard to keep an info-gathering collar on the neck of a big male—the neck is frequently almost as large as its head and the collars slip off. Ear tags help in identification; however, they are frequently torn out in altercations with other males.

All this said, Woofie was as large as any bear I'd seen at McNeil— I'd estimate his weight was eight hundred to a thousand pounds that June. With a dark chocolaty-brown coat and without visible scars, Woofie was just plain big and beautiful.

When I first spotted him, he appeared shy and seemed to choose to stay away from people. I can remember watching him from hundreds of yards away, running back and forth, in and out of cover, as if he was very agitated. Anthropomorphically speaking, it was as if he wanted to get closer but couldn't muster up the courage. Eventually he did venture closer and the running back and forth changed to short hop charges of a few steps toward us, before turning and retreating.

Again, a "hop" charge is a short head-down rush of a few feet toward an adversary—in this case, my group and me. While such a charge looks threatening, it usually happens after an interaction with people has taken place and is at a safe—to me, not the bear—distance. They are not uncommon and usually a male thing.

It took Woofie a few summers to stop moving away from people. It's impossible to say that he began to be at ease, but during these same years, he became the obvious alpha male at McNeil and few bears challenged him. Those who did so never tried more than once. He was the most aggressive bear I'd ever seen. Never in my ten years at McNeil and in the countless encounters I witnessed did I see him be anything but the dominant bear.

Since age five or six, I've been an *Iliad* and *Odyssey* buff. Being ran in the family. My grandmother liked Hector and Andromache, and so she sided with the Trojans. She thought the sacking of Troy and the killing of Hector and Andromache's son Astyanax was one of the saddest events in literature. My mother went for Athena, and thus the Greeks and Odysseus, as the gray-eyed goddess favored both. For me, Achilles, the ultimate Greek hero, was my favorite.

When Woofie arrived at the McNeil River Falls for his daily fishing, it was similar to Achilles approaching Troy to avenge the death of his friend Patroclus by the hand of Hector. All scattered before him. When Woofie approached, all the other bears got out of his way. If they weren't quick about it, a fight could ensue—he didn't spend time on formalities.

Sex for Woofie was another thing. At first we never saw him actually mate, but we did see him fight over and follow females. But f*ck he did not. I like to think of Woofie hanging with his friends in the evening. When they'd ask, "What kind of day did you have Woofie?" He'd say, "Only a 2F day, I just followed and fought." When he eventually had a 3F day, I'm not sure if he related the fact to anyone.

Here are some Woofie observations from my field notes for a single day in July of 1993.

Woofie standing and rubbing against alders at his favorite rubbing spot at edge of meadow—drawing alders through mouth—holding against face with front paws—did not see the behavior that led to the rubbing.

20 minutes later—Woofie moving toward and mating for 20 minutes with Teddy—bit Teddy on both sides of face—broke apart—she moved off going out of sight—he followed.

Woofie appears again on riverbank. Very tolerant of smaller male—jaws at him. ["Jawing" is a midlevel opened-mouth threat that very seldom leads to contact. Commonly seen between females as threatening displays, as warnings to one another to keep your distance. Al Stokes coined the phrase.] Other bear moves off fifty feet and lies down.

Woofie and two other big males stand and rub on same spot as Woofie rubbed earlier—over a period of about 60 minutes. One bear rubbed for about 35 seconds.

Woofie seen mating with Helen on far ridge. [No duration noted.] Medium male sits 100 feet away. [One of four different bears seen mating with Helen in two days.]

## Another July day:

Woofie approaches fishing Earl [large male as big as Woofie and who is fishing in the most productive fishing spot at McNeil Falls]—Woofie approaches then lowers and twists head—Earl backs up and moves off 50 feet and cowboy walks for about 30 seconds, peeing all over himself—Woofie moves into spot and immediately catches fish—eats in place.

Creek Bear runs away from approaching Woofie. Woofie gives off no signals I can identify, other than directly approaching.

Woofie and Harley interaction [Harley is a big male that appears slightly larger than Woofie]: Woofie came down bank [far side of river from where I was sitting]. Harley [who was actively fishing] turned and faced Woofie for a moment. Open mouths. Touched? [No time written down.] Harley then pushed Woofie with front paw. Woofie moved forward. Both bears had mouth's open. [River noise blocks possible sound from that distance.] Harley had canines covered. Couldn't see Woofie's because of sight angle. Harley's ears back and flat. Woofie's forward. Harley backed while facing. Woofie turned and took over Harley's fishing spot. Harley moved 15 feet and lay down.

Woofie fishing and catching five chums. Then sitting in #1 fishing spot and facing cowboy walking Sterling (big male).

I enjoyed every second I spent watching Woofie. And he calmed down over the years. On many occasions, he allowed groups to come close. He was, however, most of the time, a far-side, opposite-riverbank bear, fishing and resting in the alders over there.

Woofie was still at McNeil when I left in 2000. I'm not sure what happened to him and when he stopped being the alpha male. I hope he didn't "go to Texas" as we sometimes sadly say when a bear is shot. That's when some yahoo shoots a bear, gets it stuffed, and proudly displays it in their trophy room in Dallas. One moment of instant and selfish gratification traded for the life of an intelligent animal.

Another peninsula brown bear ended up in the pharmacy of the town closest to where I grew up. The owner was an avid trophy hunter and had gone to Alaska to "blast" a bear. Today you can book combination trips to Alaska that are actually called "Blast and Cast." Blast a bear and cast for a fish.

Anyway, the pharmacist could have hunted in any number of places, but a guide took him to Lake Becharof where he got "a big one." I was startled the first time I walked into the store and was confronted by the trophy bear mounted full sized, standing upright with mouth open and plastic teeth exposed in what the taxidermist must have thought was a fearsome snarl. Placed in one giant paw was a sign reading: "Had a Grizzly Experience? Try Prozac."

• • •

While working for the state at McNeil, I obtained a special permit for Daniel Zatz, an Emmy Award–winning cinematographer from Homer, to come in and photograph with the intention of jointly producing a film about bear behavior.

It had been more than twenty years since I made the films with Howie. Instead of shooting in 16 mm, Daniel recorded in digital format. With film, you have to be selective in your shots; with digital, you can shoot everything. And this what we did. Eventually we produced a short film, *Way of the Bear in Alaska*, which, some twenty years after its debut, continues to sell and rent to individuals, universities, and film libraries.

Daniel is a great photographer and film editor, and our film won several prizes. We won first prize from the North American Outdoor Writer's Association Film Festival. This award means the film was a hit with the general public. The science-oriented Animal Behavior Society is on the other end of the spectrum. (Allen Stokes was one of the founders.) We took second prize at their yearly film festival. The film's judges were research scientists. We also received Best Educational and Best Biological Information Film awards at the prestigious International Film Festival in Missoula, Montana, where we were up against major filmmakers. I felt a strong validation for my work on the social behavior and communication of bears.

· · ·

I left the sanctuary in 2000. I realized private guiding would be more rewarding both spiritually and financially than being at McNeil where everything was regimented. I could again be the boss, set my own hours, and wander where I wanted. I could go to places where it would be just me, one or two clients, and the bears.

That's how I have spent nearly the last twenty years. Private guiding has given me the opportunity to view new landscapes and behavior. I continue to learn. Sure it's the same tribe of bears, but having the opportunity to see new individuals coping with different environments and each other is endlessly fascinating.

However, more than this, being on my own gave me the opportunity to meet new people who had entered the guide business and were genuinely interested in the different things they were seeing each day.

Sharing in the excitement and curiosity bear guides Ken and Chris Day and Dave Bachrach had with bears was going full circle. Back to when Molly and I talked endlessly about animals' minds with Sykes and Juan in Vermont, with Howie at Becharof as we all learned to work around bears, or with Al Stokes and my two helpers at McNeil, Jeff Nelson and Ron Spry, as we tried to figure out the world of bears.

Being away from McNeil exposed me to the best wildlife cinematographers from all around the world and allowed me to get them shots that because of regulations were impossible at McNeil. I quickly learned the advantages of remote-controlled cameras, which could be set out and then operated from a distance, keeping human disturbance to bears at a minimum. Underwater shots, something also not allowed at McNeil, taken with high-speed underwater cameras showed me that a bear's world didn't end, like mine, at the water's edge, but that they knew the stream bottoms every bit as well as the trails on dry land.

Now each bear trip is different. A day seldom goes by when I don't see something new. Fish runs start and come to an end, sedges die, berries ripen, seasons come and go, and the great bears move through them as they always have.

# 19

## Where the Bears Are

In fact, a narrow concept of habitat may be inapplicable for bears, which are wide-ranging creatures of the landscapes rather than habitat types per se.

—J. Schoen

oday when I take people bear watching, I go to where the food is. That's where the bears are. I start my season in May in coastal meadows where plants are beginning to become green and nutritious. For good viewing, I want bears, good visibility, and easy walking.

One way to learn about bears is to understand their nutritional needs. Quite simply, brown bears have developed a strategy of putting on enough weight when food is available to survive when it isn't.

During the first two weeks in June, the first salmon runs begin and many bears abandon the sedges. So do I. After having spent a month in the estuaries and clam flats, it's wonderful to be able to watch bears catching fish.

Bears are salmon gourmets and Alaska gives them five species to choose from: sockeye or red; coho or silver; chum, keta, or dog; pink or humpy; and king, also called Chinook, blackmouth, or spring. They seem to prefer the high fat content of kings and reds, but these two species are not always available. I've seen bears wade through streams bursting with hundreds of spawning pinks to grab, then eat a chum that had wandered into the mix.

I'm like a bear myself, preferring kings and reds. Interspersed with halibut, we eat them all winter. If there is nothing else, I'll eat a fresh silver. Chums? I ate enough at McNeil to last me forever.

Pinks, because they are so delicate, are okay if they are fried up for dinner the night you catch them.

Salmon runs vary widely from year to year. There can be almost complete failures in returns. When this happens the bears go elsewhere seeking out streams where there are fish. Likewise for berry crops. If there are no berries in an area, which happens, the bears move on looking for better patches.

A dead sea lion weighing more than half a ton washed up on the beach in front of the McNeil camp. Bears are supposed to eat dead sea mammals, and I've seen them eating dead harbor seals. Anyway, with at least fifty McNeil bears in the immediate area, one would have thought that very quickly one would be feasting. Not so, a few bears walked up and gave it a sniff, then continued on their way. A few others slowly approached to within a few feet, then looking frightened took off running down the beach. An occasional eagle stopped by, but apparently the thick skin of the sea lion was too much for even a sharp beak.

It wasn't until we cut out some pieces of hide to send to the government as samples of this particular protected marine mammal that things began to happen. Still no bears but the eagles landed and began to enlarge the holes we had started. Then one morning I looked out and lying on top of the sea lion was a small bear. He had the whole fifteen-hundred-pound carcass to himself until a few days later growing tides floated his meal away. Why was he the only bear that ate the sea lion? How come bears don't always do like they are supposed to?

Nothing draws in bears more than a dead whale. Judging by how much time they spend eating, it must be as good as it gets for a bear— blubber to be converted to blubber with minimal effort, except to tell an adversary now and then to move over. One year I had to stop taking people to Tutuk Creek because all the bears had abandoned salmon and gone north a few miles to eat twenty or thirty tons of humpback whale.

Whatever the bears are eating, summer is a time for feeding and for dramatic gains in weight. While salmon seems to be the preferred food of coastal brown bears, the availability of berries in late summer and fall tempts them away to the hillsides.

One plant I've never had much luck watching brown bears eat is devil's club (*Oplopanax horridus*). But I know they eat lots of it as evidenced by the berry seeds in their droppings. On a moose hunting trip about fifteen miles north of Tutuk Creek, I found a patch of devil's club hundreds of acres in size, by far the largest I'd ever experienced. Every so often along the edges I'd see where brown bears had made paths into this dense stand. Because the devil's club grew higher than a walking bear and hung down over path entrances, the trails took on the look of dark tunnels. There could have been a hundred bears in the place and I wouldn't have seen a one. It was definitely a bear's world in there.

I've rarely seen big males eating berries when salmon are available. Male bears are very big bodied and it may be that expending energy eating and wandering looking for berries isn't efficient—more energy goes out to feeding than goes into fat for the winter. They get more bang for the buck when they subsist on salmon.

I've always suspected that younger bears, because they were growing, as well as pregnant and lactating females had different nutritional needs than mature males. I'd guess that while berries offer carbohydrates, proteins, and sugar, they likely have other beneficial nutrients not found in salmon. Also, when big males are down on the creeks eating salmon, berry-covered hillsides are good places for less dominant bears to be.

Some bears obviously like to make the best of both worlds. During the fall months bears continue to go for the most nutritious foods. At Moraine Creek and Becharof, I've seen bears, especially subadults and young females, alternate between snacking on berries for a few hours then going back to the creeks to scavenge for late spawning and dead salmon.

However, all bears don't do the same thing at the same time. Bears are both individuals and opportunists. In the summer of 2015, many bears, including mature males, left salmon streams and rivers to take advantage of the biggest and earliest berry crops anyone could remember. Not only were bears feasting on blueberries (*Vaccinum uliginosum*) and crowberries (*Empetrum nigrum*), which had matured weeks early thanks to an early spring and warm summer, but their scat showed the distinct seeds of devil's club berries in late July instead of the typical late August.

In September I take my clients to watch bears move between berry patches and salmon streams. This is my favorite time of year. In the higher elevations of Katmai National Park Preserve, colors are changing and if a bear can be playing in the tundra, eating berries, and catching a late run red or early silver salmon, these are indeed fat, happy bears.

• • •

When bears aren't eating or searching for food, they are resting. It makes sense. Why put on weight only to run it off? It's a big part of a bear's life.

Since my first days at Becharof, I've always noted where these resting places were. I soon learned that the use and placement of these spots was far from random. And understanding where these places were and how they were used gave insight into the society of bears.

Subadults tended to rest where they could see other bears coming. Mothers and cubs also picked areas with good visibility, like in the middle of a muskeg flat or on a very wide beach. I soon learned a subadult lying on the lakeshore at Becharof or on the beach at Kamishak Bay might have been enjoying the gentle breezes or perhaps the absence of bugs, but assuredly had picked his or her spot so escape was possible should a larger bear come along.

Big males do lots of resting in heavy cover, although sometimes they plop down most anywhere. When I could observe them, they often appeared dead to the world. My Becharof notes tell of having a brown bear and a bald eagle in sight at one time. Both were resting when I first saw them—and both were still resting when I left them seven hours later. The eagle never left its perch, nor the bear his bed. I imagine they were both satiated after an earlier salmon feast.

Subadults and females constantly raise their heads while dilating their nostrils as they apparently look and smell for approaching bears—presumably the occasionally predatory and obviously feared big males.

The bluffs at the bottom of Mikfik Creek at McNeil River are used by subadults, single females, and mothers with cubs. Some of the resting places in the bluffs are in spots so steep bears have to back down to get to them. I have seen big males get very interested in these bears. They'll lean over the bear or bears below but seem reluctant to turn around to descend. The bottom bear can bite and use front paws and claws to defend itself while the descending bear can offer nothing except for a vulnerable backend. Likewise, if a bear should try to approach from below the above bear can lean down and bite and hit at its defenseless face and head.

Somewhere along the line resting spots become bear beds, like the ones I looked over with the Scott family near the Ephraim River. Repeated use and digging turn simple resting spots into features in the landscape. There are beds on the bluffs on the upper stretches of Funnel Creek in Katmai National Park used by both females and sub-adults. There is usually one way in and one way out of these promontories. There are also nearby escape routes the bears know about, down steep rock shoots to the creek some seventy to eighty feet below.

It doesn't take much time to realize that only large males are resting and eating in the beds tucked among the alders and willows within a few feet of Moraine Creek also in Katmai. All you have to do is sit on the bank and watch them move from water to bed and bed to water.

One rarely meets big males in the tundra above the creek. These big guys seem to find a place easy to catch salmon and prefer to camp out on the closest dry ground. Again an example of energy efficiency.

The alders immediately around the McNeil River Falls also seem to be the province of big males, with other bears picking resting spots where they can defend themselves or see an adversary away from the falls.

It's not a perfect world. Once I saw a big male with his eyes closed, lying motionless in a prone position on a riverbank, presumably having a rest after a stressful day of killing salmon. (Al Stokes would have said I couldn't really say he was asleep, but . . .) As he lay there another bear came along and without any precursors made a lunge and sunk his teeth into in the middle of his back—and held on. It took a few seconds for the resting bear to break his attacker's grip and turn to face the bigger bear.

• • •

Where the bears are fishing gives us clues to the social stratification in brown bear society. It's actually pretty simple. The most dominant bears get the best fishing spots, and they know where the best spots are. If you went to McNeil and there was only one bear there, you can be assured it would be in the most productive spot.

This is true of who gets best access to other food sources. Best sedges in Kukak Bay—most dominant males. Best razor clam beds at Hallo Bay—most dominant males. Best fishing spot in the shallow water off the mouth of Tutuk Creek—most dominant males. And so on.

• • •

Some, but certainly not all, bears spend parts of their lives on Cook Inlet and Shelikof Strait shores and parts on different Bristol Bay drainages. Bears are long legged—designed to move and explore different habitats.

My samples of bear movements are very small. Here's why: The fact that I saw thirteen bears in a two-mile stretch heading west in the rocky alpine pass between McNeil River and Moraine Creek in early August objectively means nothing more than I saw thirteen bears, headed west, out of an airplane window on a bear trail between McNeil and Moraine Creek.

However, "The bear went over the mountain, the bear went over the mountain . . ."

These bears were going over the mountain to where there was more, easy-to-get, high-quality food in the form of red salmon.

When Jon Berryman and I counted the thirteen bears out of the window of his airplane, I knew the chum salmon run at McNeil was ending, and at the same time, Bristol Bay red salmon, which I've mentioned are part of the world's largest salmon run, were beginning to enter spawning streams on the Bristol Bay side of the Aleutian Mountains.

I also knew bear numbers at McNeil peaked in mid-July and dropped to just a few by mid-August—obviously, the bears had to go somewhere. Likewise, Lake Becharof, again on the Bristol Bay side, had few bears in late May and early June, while the sedge flats over the mountains to the east along Shelikof Strait were full of bears.

Bears tranquilized and marked in Kukak Bay on Shelikof Strait during the Exxon Valdez oil spill in 1989 showed up at McNeil River the same summer almost seventy miles away. Bears I marked with the ADF&G at McNeil were killed by hunters in the Katmai Preserve, over the mountains and some thirty miles to the west. McNeil bears have been spotted at Brooks Falls in Katmai National Park, and bears marked in the southern sections of Katmai near Hallo Bay have moved to the northern edge of Lake Becharof. Some bears fish both McNeil River and Tutuk Creek during July, covering the ten miles between the watersheds in only a few hours.

• • •

Fall in Alaska marks the onset of two major events: bad weather and hunting season. I've always stopped guiding by the beginning of October as flying, which is so critical to my operation, can become outright dangerous due to fog and storms.

While everything is beautiful—the bears amble in their new winter coats, and I dream of lying on a Hawaiian beach—a dark specter lurks. Guide camps pop up along salmon streams and hunters in full camo wander through the Anchorage airport—the bear hunt is set to begin. More than twelve hundred brown bears, including some I have been watching all summer, are about to meet their end.

• • •

My mother described shooting a rhino. She said you get out in the open, wave your arms, and get the rhino to charge toward you. At the last minute, you step out of its way and shoot it slightly below the ear as it thunders past. To get a big brownie, hide in the alders until it enters the water to get a fish, quickly move close to the bank and either shoot him in the water or when he's climbing the bank. Of course, now with modern firearms—including high-powered sniper rifles—there is no need to get very close.

# 20

## Ages and Stages

**S**olstice was a long-time resident of Tutuk Creek, about ten miles north of the McNeil Sanctuary. She was the queen of the hop and year after year the most dominant female on the stream. In 2001, when I first saw her, she was known to have already raised and weaned a litter of cubs. She was easy to distinguish from other bears as she was almost white in color, had a characteristic Roman nose, and was bigger than any other female in the area. She was so distinctive I could show her to a visitor and forever after they could identify her.

One June morning, not long ago, I realized Solstice was missing. Salmon were starting to show up in the stream and for the previous eighteen years she'd always been there when the first fish arrived. I was worried, thinking some brave nimrod might have shot her the previous hunting season. Over the years she'd given birth to litter after litter of cubs and her loss would have been tragic, not only for the additions she would continue to make to the population of Tutuk Creek bears, but also for me and a few other people who had come to regard her as their favorite bear.

Happily, a few days later I spotted a light-colored bear high on a mountainside a mile away from where I was sitting next to the creek. With the aid of my spotting scope, I could see it was Solstice. To my delight she had three tiny cubs with her.

The family stayed in an area of steep rock cliffs and I suspected she was keeping the cubs away from other bears. As I watched she rested near various steep rock outcroppings, which looked like locations she could escape to. She was far from the first female with cubs I'd seen resting and grazing in hard-to-reach places.

Except for her cubs, Solstice was alone for three more days. Then, without any warning, the whole family came down to the creek, staying for the rest of the summer—despite the presence of several big males in the small place where the salmon were vulnerable to bears. When she did come down, she literally ran for a mile as a big school of loudly splashing fish entered the stream from salt water—my notes say she immediately caught and ate nine.

Did hunger overcome her protective mode? Very likely. But all I really know is she alternately rested and fished next to Tutuk Creek until the salmon run ended a month later, tolerating big males to about a hundred feet. Regardless of her motivation, I was certainly happy to see her.

• • •

Solstice, like other Alaska brown bears, gave birth to these cubs in a winter den during January or February. At birth the cubs weighed about a pound. They nursed, grew quickly, and stayed in the den with Solstice until April or May. When they emerged, they weighed fifteen to twenty-five pounds and were completely reliant on their mother to provide food and protection. When I first saw Solstice's cubs in the rocks, they would have been about five months old and out of their winter home for roughly two months.

During their first summer most of these small bears are dark brown, although colors range to blond, light brown, and sometimes a beautiful silver gray. All the cubs in a litter aren't necessarily the same color. I don't know why most are dark or why some cubs have white collars around their necks. Solstice's cubs seem to have a preponderance for these bands.

A classical ethologist might ask if there was survival value in being dark colored or having a white collar. I've often wondered but have never been able to answer this question. The collars are usually, but not always, gone by the time the cubs turn two. However, sometimes I've seen mature bears with faint white markings around their necks—remnant "cub collars."

• • •

First-year cubs are referred to as "cubs of the year"—or the acronym COY—by some, and as "spring cubs" by others. I like the latter term as it has a nice ring and makes me think of beginnings. (I've tossed "COY" out with the terms "boar" and "sow," as bears are not pigs.) These young bears tend to keep close to their mother, but as they mature wander farther and farther from her. There is a direct correlation between the age of cubs and the distance they roam from their mothers. She is usually, but not always, the leader when the family moves from place to place. This is a handy fact to know when going into bear country. Spring cubs are apt to walk or run behind their mother and thus you are likely to meet the mom before you meet the cubs. Not so with yearlings and older cubs, who are beginning to range and explore and may meet you before you encounter the mom.

Early in the summer, females with spring cubs may be intolerant of other bears; however, they are far more likely to lead their young offspring away from aggressive situations rather than into them.

I've seen females with spring cubs break off aggressive displays to dash away and gather up fleeing cubs. There's always the spring cub who gets right up there with its mother, deciding it wants to see if it can intimidate another bear. I've been charged by these little bears. When they break away from their mother and come at you, these charges are a short rush of a step or two. It would appear the farther you get from your mother the less courage you have.

As cubs go, Solstice's latest three tended to be highly aggressive. Of course, they had her six-hundred-pound bulk backing them up. One theory, common in other species and one that I'd love to investigate in bears, asks this question: Do aggressive mothers have aggressive offspring? I suspect they do.

Mothers and cubs are something to be respected and given plenty of room if you should happen to surprise them. Mother bears have been known to act defensively. It doesn't mean you will be attacked, but *if* the mother doesn't depart the area, you may receive a few threats to remind you to keep your distance. Sometimes it takes a mom what seems like an age to get things figured out. You want a New York minute; she's on bear time. Anyway, her figuring things out—or whatever she is doing behind those dark eyes—can make for a very long moment, one that drags on and on and on. It's good to remember that she maybe has your number and is only pulling your chain.

Now, meeting a cub who has ranged away from its mother is another experience that can be stressful. If the cub becomes frightened, it can trigger a response in the mother, as she is apt to pick up on the behavior of the cub rather than on perceived danger. The cub gets excited, the mom gets excited, and the next thing you know you are surrounded by upset bears.

When Solstice appeared one spring, Clyde was her only cub. Had she given birth to only one? Or had she lost another one, two, or even three? Regardless, Clyde was a terror. He'd stay close to Solstice when she fished, taking bites of whatever she caught, but whenever another bear passed by, he'd made miniature charges, with ears back and mouth open, then quickly retreat and press up against the fishing Solstice. Sometimes, without moving from where she was sitting or standing she'd turn her head in the direction of what he was bothering, giving the impression she was a mother bored with her child—"Come on, kid, cut it out and let me keep eating."

Clyde never put a rush on any mature bears, only cubs and sub-adults. If a big male got anywhere near, he'd snuggle up alongside or even duck underneath Solstice.

There's a lot of touching—tactile stimulation—between mother and offspring. This behavior may be initiated by either the cubs or the mother, particularly after periods of separation or stressful situations. Placing one or both front feet against her, standing or crouching underneath, or simply resting up against their mother are common sights.

Much of the variation in behavior of females with spring cubs is determined by age, social rank, and availability of food. Does she have enough social standing to move other bears? If she does, she may range a short distance from her cubs. If the female is young and low on the social ladder, she may keep extremely close to the cubs and they to her. Different females act in different ways in different situations. A hungry female may move into a perilous position near a possibly predatory male in order to get a meal of salmon.

Occasionally, I have seen spring cubs traveling short distances on their mother's back. One female at Becharof had a single cub that would regularly jump up on her back when she made threatening lunges to keep other bears at a distance.

Another June, on Tutuk Creek, a female appeared with four spring cubs—a rare sight. She hung around and fished for three days but was eventually spooked by the approach of a large male and ran off with all four cubs. She was soon out of sight in high grass and alders and for the next hour or so we could hear the bawling cries of the cubs from different spots as the family, obviously separated, tried to get back together.

Several hours later she reappeared with only two cubs. She fished for a few hours each day for the next two days, the two cubs staying close. On the third day she had all four cubs back, but three days later she appeared with only two. Over the next few weeks, she only had two and the following year she had two yearlings.

When cubs get separated, their calls not only attract their mothers but also other bears—including mature males. Watching mothers look for lost cubs or cubs looking for their moms is incredibly nerve-racking and makes me as stressed as I ever get watching bears. I'd rather have a subadult making hop charges toward me than watch an obviously distraught mother race around trying to pick up the scent trail of her lost offspring.

For the most part, female bears do the fishing for their spring cubs and in many cases for their yearlings. Contrary to popular belief, they do not stand on the stream bank and swat passing fish up on the bank for the cubs to eat. I have yet to see this phenomenon, but maybe someday on a spawning stream in Bristol Bay, I'll have the chance.

Far more common is for the mother to catch a fish and as she eats, she'll allow the cubs to grab and tear off what they can. As she fills up, she leaves scraps and there is more available for the cubs to eat. When she begins to be satiated and is only taking a bite out of the head, eating strips of skin, or eggs if she has captured a female, the cubs dig into almost the entire fish.

The main thing here is that female bears don't share. They don't present food to their offspring. She allows them to eat what she is eating, even allowing her cubs to take partially eaten fish away, but they must come to her and take or grab what they can. Nor do the cubs share with each other. Raucous cub fights over scraps are a daily and entertaining occurrence.

The availability of salmon, water levels, and the density of bears on a stream all affect the ability of spring cubs to catch fish. McNeil River Falls is a tough spot and one can sit here for days and not see a spring or yearling cub be successful. On other shallow streams up the coast, particularly in a strong fish run, spring cubs can catch swimming salmon. While they seem to prefer grabbing what they can from their mother, they can and do get fish on their own. At spawning streams on Lake Becharof, where the salmon are almost thick enough to walk on, fishing for these small bears is easy and their success rate is very high. They can create carnage in spawning beds, picking up, biting, and dropping salmon as their predatory behavior continues long after they are full of fish.

Imagine the scene: A forty-pound cub fighting to keep a ten-pound Bristol Bay red salmon in its mouth using baby teeth. In spite of repeatedly dropping and picking up again, the cubs usually win. Even at this young age, bears are efficient predators.

· · ·

Cubs stay with their mother through the first summer and den with her in late October or early November. They have grown incredibly and may weigh 150 pounds or more. In late April or May they emerge again to spend spring, summer, and fall with her. These young bears are referred to as yearlings. The family travels together, the cubs still nursing, but otherwise eating the same foods as their mother. Yearlings may aggressively approach cubs from other families, as well as recently weaned subadults and even people.

Of all age classes of bears, yearling cubs are the most interesting to watch. They've gone from being babies to little bears and are constantly in motion as they approach other small bears, investigate anything and everything, and constantly play with each other, their mother, and things they discover: sticks, logs, dead fish, and new objects humans throw away that come in with the tide—Styrofoam, rubber fishing buoys, plastic water bottles, shoes, ropes . . . They chase, but seldom catch, pretty much anything that isn't a bear, such as gulls, eagles, ground squirrels, sparrows, warblers, ptarmigan, and foxes.

They wander away from their mother for greater distances than they did when they were spring cubs but still run back to her protection if things don't go their way. The last refuge for a yearling bear is with its mother.

The average litter size for Alaska Peninsula brown bears is two or three cubs. Based on what I've seen, a very small sample size, my guess is females start to lose cubs in the first few months. While I occasionally see females with four spring cubs, only once have I seen a mother with four yearlings.

On a rare blue-sky, sixty-degree day at Lake Becharof with light westerlies and calm seas, Howie, Molly, and I decided to forgo a day on Cleo Creek, take the skiff part way east down the lake, and hike past the base of Mount Peulik and down toward Ugashik Lake. We didn't get far. About two miles in we came upon a mother with four yearlings lying on a hillside looking like they were watching our every move.

It turned into one of my most memorable days. We filmed and watched for hours with Ugashik visible to the south, Becharof to the north, to the west the vast coastal plain of the peninsula extending to the horizon, and rising immediately to the east, the massive form and steep slopes of the smoking Mount Peulik.

As the bears fed on berries and moved over a ridge, we followed. When they'd rest, we'd rest. Then they'd move over another ridge, we'd follow, they'd graze, we'd eat. Sunshine, warmth, fair skies, five bears, smoking volcanoes in an untouched place—a great day! And the only time I have ever seen a female with four yearlings.

A friend, who spends lots of time on the Alaska Peninsula, watched a female raise four cubs to weaning as two-year-olds. After leaving the cubs, the female mated. The next year she was observed with three spring cubs. At some point during that summer, with her new family in tow, she picked up another "runty" spring cub for a total of four. She successfully kept all four through the winter and then appeared in the spring with four yearlings. Some bear!

Some females turn out cubs like clockwork every three years, others don't seem to be able to keep their cubs through the first summer— just like humans, there are apparently good and bad mothers.

• • •

In the fall of the cub's second year, the family once again dens together. By this time cubs may weigh more than 250 pounds and are bigger than most black bears. When the family emerges in the spring, the cubs are two and a half years old. They continue to nurse, which can look very odd—especially if the mother is small and she has three cubs almost as big as she is.

For the most part, the cubs stay near the female; however, starting in May, sometimes sooner and sometimes later, the mother comes into estrus, and instead of being intolerant of large males, she begins to allow them to approach.

Many use the term "family breakup" to describe the event of a bear family separating. It's really not the best term as it sounds absolute and paints a picture that's not correct. Certainly, life is altered and takes on a new direction with mother and cubs going their separate ways, but this phenomenon doesn't end their relationship. It simply marks a time of change.

During this transition, several things are happening. The female is undergoing hormonally induced behavioral changes typical of carnivores, and the cubs are now able to find food for themselves and for the most part know how to act independently in social situations.

A mother may simply ignore her cubs or even chase them if they come close; however, the mere presence of the male often seems to be enough to keep the cubs away. It looks to be a stressful time for the young bears, what with having to run away from other bears and not having a mother to protect them, or catch fish, or lead from berry patch to berry patch. The cubs look lost for a few days but then seem to settle quickly into their new motherless roles.

After she is out of estrus, commonly two or three weeks, she is intolerant of her own cubs, biting and chasing if they get too close. She seems equally intolerant to any other subadults should they come near.

But bears are individuals with a range of behaviors that are exceptions to the norms.

One year on May 30, I saw a female accompanied by a pair of two-and-a-half-year-old cubs. I knew how old they were because I had seen them repeatedly as spring cubs and yearlings. They were easy to identify, a dark brown male and a much lighter female. The mother nursed them in the morning and abandoned them in the afternoon, taking off with a male with whom I saw her mating several days later. On June 17 the female, unlike most bears who have become intolerant, was back with the cubs and again nursed them. The family stayed together until mid-August when they left the area. This story doesn't have a satisfactory ending. I never saw the mother again, nor was I able to identify the cubs the next summer.

But, while the majority of families seem to separate at the beginning of the cub's third summer, this is not how it works for Solstice and for two of her offspring that have given birth to cubs of their own. Solstice has always kept her cubs for three summers, and now her cubs Scrappy and Stella continue in the family tradition, keeping their cubs through a third summer. I have no explanation for this. All three did it as young mothers and continued in subsequent litters.

• • •

Cub mortality is high, many die in the first three years of life. Females usually mature at four to seven years of age. If she breeds at six, gives birth at seven, has cubs every three years, and goes on having cubs until her midtwenties, she'll have six litters during her lifetime. Two and a half cubs per litter equals fifteen cubs. Half of the litter would be male and half female, of which 50 percent won't survive. So with luck she places seven or eight new cubs into the population over her lifetime, only three or four being females. Add in human-caused mortality, which is usually 4 to 8 percent of heavily hunted populations like the Alaska Peninsula, and you can see a female doesn't replace herself in the population many times.

Because she keeps her cubs for an extra year, Solstice would add even fewer cubs to the population. Thought to have vanished when she was about age twenty-five, she would have only given birth to five litters, with luck perhaps adding two or three females to the bears of Tutuk Creek.

I've seen mothers abandon cubs that had been grabbed by males, but on two occasions I've observed mothers furiously attacking males who had pinned cubs to the ground and were obviously intent on killing. "Hell hath no fury" like the unbelievably swift and savage attack of a mother bear. Both times the male was forced to drop the cub. And in both instances the cubs survived.

In one of these episodes, the female grabbed the male who was approximately twice her size by the hind leg, the appendage nearest to her. In a split second, she went from his leg to his head, making bites too fast to see. Muhammad Ali could fire off four jabs in a second. Watch a fight and his glove becomes a blur. A bear can bite at least this quickly. The female's onslaught was enough to make the male back off, blood streaming from multiple wounds.

An encounter Solstice had over a cub was shorter in duration but no less fierce. As she fished, her cub wandered too close to a big opportunistic male. Within seconds the male grabbed the cub, the cub shrieked, Solstice charged, hitting him broadside, with head down and mouth open, completely knocking him off his feet. He dropped the cub and spent several seconds trying to get his feet back underneath him, as Solstice made multiple bites on his face and head. When he again got upright, he backed off and she stopped her assault but continued to threaten him.

If there is something more violent than a bear attack, I've never seen it. I can't imagine anything other than a bear standing up to one.

While these were uncommon occurrences, males do kill cubs. The fact they do likely accounts for much of the behavior females show toward other bears, particularly males. But I don't know how this phenomenon contributes to the high mortality rate of young bears.

I once saw a cub killed in late August, well past the normal mating season. In two other cases I saw males kill cubs, taking one of two and the other time one of three. In these cases I did not see the female come into estrus as a result of the mortality, nor did I see her with new cubs the next spring.

Many people think males kill cubs so females will come into estrus, mate with the male, and thus the male gets to place his genes into the population. This idea likely comes from their interpretation of the behavior of African lions transposed to bears—if lions kill cubs so do bears. It would be difficult to set up an experiment to see if this is true.

First you'd have to find and get a DNA sample from a mother with cubs. This would mean immobilizing and taking a blood or hair sample. Then you'd have to witness a male bear killing her cubs. This would mean closely monitoring the mother with cubs to make certain you were there to witness the event. And this could take a while as years go by at McNeil with no cub killing at all. Then you'd have to immobilize the guilty male and get a DNA sample. Then the next year you'd have to again find the female, immobilize her newborn cubs and check to see if the parent was the male who killed the previous litter. Of course, if you had a bunch of bears previously marked and had their DNA samples you could check on which males were represented in the cub population. But if you hadn't witnessed exactly who killed the cubs, what would you be proving?

I've had more than one person say to me in defense of their killing a big male, "You know, if we kill big males, we get more bears, because big males kill so many cubs."

We have a long way to go.

# 21

## Bonds and Maturity

After family breakup occurs, young subadult bears are likely to share their mother's home range—at least for a year or two. Once they're weaned and abandoned, subadult siblings tend to stay together. They play and tolerate one another as they catch salmon or graze on vegetation. They frequently move other bears away from the best fishing spots by displaying together as a cohesive unit. Even at this age of two or three, the more aggressive behavior of males is becoming apparent, with young males becoming the leaders of these gangs of two or three bears.

Solstice's cubs are likely to be a year older at weaning than other cubs. The payoff is obvious when you watch these young bears of Tutuk Creek. Their greater size and extra experience enables them to dominate other young bears.

I haven't seen Solstice at Tutuk Creek for several years, but one of her first offspring named Scrappy is still there. One summer, not long ago, Scrappy showed up with three spring cubs. The next year all three cubs had survived and were now 150-pound yearlings. With their dominant and human-tolerant mother as back up, they routinely approached my clients and me, chased and played with subadults who were larger than they were, and caught quite a few fish, although they were still capable of stealing from easygoing Scrappy.

The next year Scrappy, like her mom keeping her cubs for a third year, appeared with three giant cubs who were estimated to weigh over two hundred pounds. They took up a lot of space, running and chasing each other and other small bears, often becoming widely separated from their mother who didn't look to be aware or care. She'd still allowed them to take her fish, occasionally nursed them, and when she left to go elsewhere they'd eventually follow. If a large male passed by, the cubs still were likely to run to her; however, they also sometimes simply moved out of harm's way.

The following year Scrappy appeared alone. A few days later what had turned into three hellions came down the creek. I had more than one "close enough" incident with them, but they eventually learned I didn't want to be part of their games and retired to a life of terrorizing other subadults and catching and eating innumerable fish.

• • •

One early morning at McNeil River, Molly and I observed a female named Jeannie who was accompanied by a pair of two-and-a-half-year-old cubs. We knew their age because Jeannie had been tranquilized and given numbered ear tags the year before. The family was together from June 14 to 16. Then they disappeared from the sedge meadow at McNeil and weren't seen together again. On July 19, more than a month after she disappeared, Jeannie reappeared as a single bear. She was then seen daily, always alone, until August 12, when she left the McNeil observation areas.

Her cubs only disappeared for a week, returning from wherever they had been on June 22, and I saw them almost daily until August 26. When Jeannie returned I didn't see the two sibs try get close to her nor did I see her chase them. During the summer we managed to immobilize both of these male cubs, give them ear tags and the names Light and Dark.

For the most part Light and Dark stayed close, frequently playing and usually moving from place to place together. When fishing, they were far more tolerant of each other than they were of other bears. They didn't go as far as sharing, but they didn't take fish from each other either. Sometimes they responded to threats as a unit, running toward or away from an adversary. If Dark played with another bear, Light frequently joined in. During the second summer I'd observed them, they'd separate for a few days but eventually get back together—sniffing, touching, and licking each other.

This sounds like a fairy tale; however, when we tranquilized Light and Dark, strange things happened. We weren't using helicopters, like most biologists today. Rather we found bears out in the open, stalked them to get close, shot them with immobilizing darts, and

followed them until they went down. When we shot Dark he col-
lapsed in a small alder patch at the edge of a meadow. Light, instead
of withdrawing from the area, chose to make loud vocalizations and
repeated charges, coming to within thirty feet of us as we measured,
placed ear tags, and took a tooth, to determine age, from the anaes-
thetized Dark. We'd yell and drive him back, only to have him return
a few minutes later, again lunging and running toward us.

This went on for about thirty minutes. Finally, Dark who had
his new ear tags and was minus a tooth, still wasn't good to go. The
drugs used in the '70s were slow acting and it took time for the
effects to wear off.

We became concerned Light or another bear might injure Dark if
we left him lying helpless, unable to defend himself. So we dragged
him out of the alders to where we could see him from a distance,
then withdrew to see if Light would come over. Thankfully he never
did, stopping all his aggressive signals once we moved away. Then
Light sat down about fifty feet from Dark, occasionally getting up
and walking short distances and then sitting down again. He never
approached his brother. After about ninety minutes Dark was up and
moved out of sight, and Light began to graze on the nearby sedges.

In 1969 an elderly female named O/D—for the olive drab collar
the Fish and Game had placed around her neck—was observed at
the McNeil River Falls. She was accompanied by three extremely
blond female yearlings. In June of 1970 all three cubs showed up
without her. Just when she weaned them is not known. We tranquilized all three of these bears naming them Red, White, and Blue,
after their respective ear tag color. During this summer the three
fished, displayed, and traveled together. Occasionally Blue would
take off for a few hours but then return. One of the three, White,
caught most of the fish for the group. She'd catch a fish, begin to eat,
and have Red and Blue descend on her aggressively tearing off and
eating what they could. During the summer of 1971, Red and Blue
were still together, acting much as they had the year before. White,
however, had taken off on her own, fished by herself, and was rarely
seen with the other two.

The bond between family members weakens as they grow older,
but I have to wonder, Does it ever completely disappear? In the

wild, without being able to identify and observe individual bears over their entire lifetimes, this is impossible to determine. If two females nurse each other's cubs, something seen one summer at McNeil, are they apt to be littermates, mother and daughter, or are they completely unrelated? Is the greeting expressed by two young males one of brotherly love or a neighborly salutation? Is the favorite play partner of an older male a sib or just a friend?

Subadult bears can be both aggressive and amiable toward bears of similar size and presumably age. They show extreme avoidance of large males—often running away at the mere sight or smell of one. They are also likely to be found in close proximity to single mature females and mothers and cubs. They are by far the most likely age class of bears to approach and even follow humans.

After I stopped working for ADF&G and left McNeil, I moved my July observations north to a small salmon stream. Sometimes I was with clients and sometimes on my own. Here I observed two cubs from the time they were yearlings until they reached the age of six. Both males, the two frequently played together. They'd sometimes separate for a day or two but always got back together. Without sign of antagonism, they were capable of fishing shoulder to shoulder. Unfortunately, one bear failed to show in the seventh summer.

As bears get older I think of them, admittedly subjectively, as young adults, akin to teenagers. My classification accounts for roughly the next three or four years of life, until the bears are five or six. I use size and behavior to place these bears. They don't act like subadults. Indeed, some in this group are of breeding age, but they don't act or have the higher places in the hierarchy of mature males or females.

On a memorable fall day in Katmai National Park Preserve, I observed and photographed six young males playing on a blueberry-covered hillside. Every bear played with every other. Where bear populations are high and hunting harvest low, such a scene is not uncommon.

Like human teenaged boys, these bears are gangly and adolescent looking. They look like they are still growing and don't yet have the size and shape of mature bears. They are still beautiful but their energy is obviously flowing into skeletal growth, not into the rounded muscle that gives mature bears their symmetrical appearance.

At this age males are taller than females and the sexes are easy to differentiate. For the most part, but certainly not always, the young males act more aggressively toward people than females.

Young males are shown little affection by females with cubs. A snooping subadult or young female may be watched carefully but a young male will be charged and chased. Adult roles become evident for the bears of this group. As they get older and larger, young adult males get closer to big males than all but the most aggressive younger subadults.

Young males just about never choose to stand up to bigger and older adversaries. It could be a good way to end up dead. Strange things do happen though. Once I saw two large males in the proximity to a female first displaying and ultimately having a knock-down, drag-out fight. A young male, less than half the size of the two big bears, snuck in and attempted to mount the female. She had nothing to do with him, as is often the case with smaller males, but he certainly tried. When the more dominant male came toward him, he retreated at a run.

The muscular stature of young bears is indicative. It isn't the same as older animals. A six-year-old male isn't nearly as large or heavy as a ten-year-old, and a four-year-old female will appear to be several hundred pounds lighter than one that is fifteen years old.

Sexual maturity for females is thought to be anywhere from as young as three to older than seven years old, with the most common age being four or five. Young males are able to breed at three or four—whether they get a chance to do so is another matter.

• • •

Mature females, like Solstice, make up two segments of the population. At times they are single females and at other times females accompanied by cubs. When they have cubs, they are protected from hunting. In the year they are pregnant and without cubs, they are fair game and legal to shoot. Each year many females turn up in "harvest" reports. Obviously, many hunters can't tell a male from a female, possibly they don't care.

Telling a male from a female is simple. If pee comes out the back end of a bear it's obviously a female; from underneath, a male. Genitals on mature males are quite apparent. There are numerous websites dedicated to telling trophy hunters how to tell the sexes apart. Perhaps high school biology would be a good place to start.

Also, male brown bears are usually bigger at a given age than females. They tend to be, but certainly not always, darker in color. Males have bigger, broader heads and thicker necks than females. Males are apt to have obvious scars on heads, necks, and front quarters. Lacerated ears and sometimes broken jaws from altercations are also easy to spot.

When fully furred, females appear far prettier, more teddy bearish, than battle-scarred males. More symmetrical and compact, they lack the rangy look of male bears. Nipples on mature females are obvious.

Hunting harvest reports list many female bears. No doubt the bigger they are, the more their trophy value. Imagine how satisfying it would be to kill an old female who had made a living in the wilderness for thirty years—successfully added cubs to the population, overcome her fear of man, and given endless hours of entertainment and pleasure to hundreds of people—brought down by a rifle shot at twenty yards as she looked up from a berry patch. Talk about hedonistic pleasure! Here's a quote from a guide in the Wrangell Mountains as we looked at the skull of an obviously old female: "Man, look how worn her teeth were, she didn't have much time left." Another from an Alaska Peninsula guide who lived in Homer: "We got this female that was so big we thought she was a male. Took four shots to kill her."

No one really knows how long bears live. Each year bears are killed that are in their late twenties. The famous wildlife biologist and conservationist Will Troyer captured and marked a bear on Kodiak Island only to have it killed by a hunter thirty-four years later. It is a simple thing for wildlife managers to say most bears die in their midtwenties. It is far more accurate to say bears in their twenties turn up in the "harvest" each year.

# 22

## Freude der Bären

John Morrow and I sat on a stream bank a few feet from the waters of Lower Cook Inlet. There was no one else around, just the way I liked it. This was our third trip together, and John, an accomplished wildlife photographer, was busy taking pictures while I gazed at the view and enjoyed the fine morning.

The ocean extended almost uninterrupted in front of us, the level horizon broken only by the smoking peak of a volcanic island some twenty miles away. All we could hear was moving water as the creek plunged over several small waterfalls and the continuous call of glaucous gulls.

Fifty feet away, fishing in shallow riffles where the freshwater met ocean salt, were two young male bears. They were catching and eating sockeye salmon, which had been attempting a final run up their natal stream to spawn. As you know, I don't like to anthropomorphize—given the difficulty of knowing the emotions of an animal—but they sure appeared to be enjoying themselves.

The German phrase "Freude der Bären" translates to "joy of bears." Sometimes I take it to mean the sheer enjoyment humans feel while watching bears, but at moments like this, I prefer simply "joyful bears" that cavort and feast when food is plentiful.

These two were Solstice's cubs, and I'd known them for seven summers. When I first spotted these cubs, I'd named them Poncho and Lefty. Lefty had stirred compassion among us humans as he alternately dragged and hobbled on a severely mangled left front paw. The injury made it difficult for him to keep up with his mother and brother and gave him his name.

So many cubs die within the first three years of life that I figured

Lefty would become a fatality. The next summer he was still there. His foot had healed but was permanently deformed.

Now the big, handsome seven-year-old walked with a pronounced limp on two toes with his heel raised in the air, rather than flat-footed like most bears. Imagine a ballerina dancing with only one toe shoe and you'll have a pretty good picture of Lefty. His gait and deformity made him easy to identify.

Poncho stood out, too. A noticeable three-inch scar ran across his chocolate-brown face, midway between the black tip of his nose and his eyes. He'd gotten his name for the mere unscientific reason it was the other half of the Townes Van Zandt song "Poncho and Lefty."

John got every image he wanted: backlit—light from behind the bears; front lit—with light from us to them; shots with salmon being caught and eaten; close-ups; and establishing shots. As we sat the bears came so close they splashed us as they chased fish. After catching twenty-one salmon (yes, I count these things—old habits die hard), Poncho and Lefty climbed the high stream bank and disappeared over the crest. John and I stayed for a few minutes to give them time to pick their next activity, then gathered up our tripods and cameras and followed.

We found the two bears playing in a muskeg meadow about a hundred yards from the creek. I knew the spot was a favorite playground and guessed they'd be there after filling up on fish.

Standing upright, perhaps eight feet tall, the two batted each other with their front paws and mouthed each other's heads and necks— they seemed oblivious to the almost continuous clicks of our electronic shutters. For an hour we watched and photographed them pushing and shoving and sometimes doing "take-downs," followed by wrestling on the ground. The bears gave no indication they were bothered by us—even when we slowly approached to within fifty feet and walked a complete circle around them, taking pictures from every conceivable angle.

It's not difficult to tell when a domesticated animal, such as a hunting dog or riding horse, is tired and perhaps needs time for itself—to rest, sleep, graze, or just get away from us. I always feel protective of animals at these moments, and it's no different with bears. So, before I think they've had enough, I leave them. It is a very subjective sentiment to have.

It had been over an hour. Though they gave us no indication we'd overstayed our welcome, we erred on the side of caution and left them still playing and ignoring us. Perhaps we could have stayed longer.

But I don't take chances.

• • •

When I started watching bears, I had no idea how much they played, what they did when they played, and who they played with. However, I did know from reading Erik Erikson and talking to my mother and Molly that if I wanted to truly understand brown bear society, I'd need to explore the phenomenon of play.

So, in a rather ironic twist, I seriously set out to study this aspect of their lives.

And I discovered that watching bears play gave me the opportunity to view their psychological and physiological development. Almost immediately, I started to form the theory that all bears, young and old, were gaining information about each other when they played. I've never wandered far from the mantra my mother practiced for a lifetime at the nursery school she founded: Learning occurs through physical play.

• • •

I set out to collect my data on play. In those first days I called it friendly physical contact. However, after months of observation, I further refined my description of play to incomplete or low intensity behavior often seen in another circumstance.

An example of this would be the wrestling match between Poncho and Lefty. It contains many of the same actions and postures you'd see in a damaging fight between two older males. Both interactions include pushing, biting, and swatting, but as I noted, when bears play, their motivation and intensity are different than when they fight for dominance.

After several years watching cubs tumbling together for a few minutes and older males pummeling each other for as long as a half hour, I surmised, but had difficulty proving, that play among bears served the critical function of reducing social stress (as it does for other species), thus allowing more time for feeding and the seasonal weight gain so critical to bears. I learned aggressive interactions rarely followed play. The bears involved grew tolerant of each other and apparently had more time to fish and graze.

Today, here's how I see it: play shapes brown bear society by building familiarity, while decreasing the ever-present threat of damage within the species.

In other words, the play behavior of bears contributes to their long and complex lives.

You may hear the term "mock fighting" to describe play. I don't use it, because it doesn't occur among the brown bears I have known. Some believe bears must "mock fight" to practice for the day when they will fight to the death for females or food. Maybe these people think ferocious bears need rehearsal time. What I've seen, however, is more clear-cut: sometimes bears play and sometimes they fight.

• • •

That first summer in Becharof, I learned that play usually starts with what I call greeting behavior, bears touch noses and mouths to each other's heads and necks. There isn't a distinct line between when greetings end and play begins. While greetings frequently lead to play, they can happen without the bears playing. When bears do greet, their ears remain upright and alert, and their facial expressions appear relaxed.

Bears, like people, have special relationships. Some bears I identified never greeted other bears I knew. There is no doubt the greeting ritual is more common between bears of similar size and sex. Large males rarely greet, rather tending to keep their distance from one another. On the rare occasion they do greet, they'll usually quickly begin to play.

Mature females seldom undergo the greeting ritual; they'll closely pass one another without touching, like strangers passing in the night. During mating season mature males and females have to become tolerant of each other—at least for short periods—so there's a lot of greeting and playing before actual coupling takes place.

Ajax has downed ten chum salmon that probably weigh seven

pounds apiece. He looks ready to throw up. As he waddles up the riverbank, he walks by Nestor, who is lying down taking a rest. As he passes, Nestor rises and stands with lowered head. Ajax turns toward him, slowly approaches, and gingerly goes nose to nose with the old bear, touching his muzzle to Nestor's head and neck. Nestor responds with a soft nip to Ajax's jowl, then a gentle push with a forepaw—and a very slow wrestling match begins.

• • •

So now you know my mantra: Individual bears do things in individual ways. However, when they play, some of the postures are common—even ritualized.

We named two of Solstice's last litter of cubs Mutt and Jeff. When they were weaned they still had a sister, but she quickly departed their company. Collectively, we'd come to know the three of them as the family from hell, because they chased, but never played with, every small bear that crossed their paths at Tutuk Creek.

As four-year-olds they behaved the same way Light and Dark had years before at McNeil. They'd separate for a day or two and then get back together. When they did they were apt to approach each other slowly swinging their heads back and forth. This predictable posturing seemed to indicate a willingness to be social. Next they'd begin to gently paw and push, then bite and nip the other's face, mouth, and neck. Once, without warning, Mutt pulled a Mike Tyson and chomped onto Jeff's ear for a few seconds, making me wince. Almost always more involved play followed this behavior.

When the two played they would frequently reverse roles. This role reversal happens often—and definitely distinguishes play from actual fighting. In their play bout, Mutt might appear to be getting the upper hand and begin to "worry" Jeff, standing over and shaking him by the throat. Then, lightning-quick, roles reverse and Jeff takes control and holds Mutt down.

This role reversal wouldn't happen in a serious altercation—if a bear backed off in a fight, the adversary could do some real damage.

At fishing sites like the McNeil River Falls, I've seen males looking for playmates approach other big males until an old pal responds and wades into the water to play. Big males often choose to play in water—maybe it supports their great bulk and makes it easier to move around.

Bears seem to know immediately when another bear only wants to play. After all, if thousand-pound Killer Joe decides he wants to play with thousand-pound Hercules, his bites and pushes are going to be refined, controlled, and deliberate. Hercules doesn't want to elicit an unwanted response from Killer Joe; he just wants to play.

I discovered one quick way to end a play bout is for me to approach the participants. All of a sudden the bears are watching the humans and play comes to a halt. For this reason I kept my distance and seldom got close enough to hear vocalizations while bears played. What I did hear was low grunting sounds and occasional farts. From a distance two playing bears are eerily silent.

• • •

Emerging from the den in April or May, first-year cubs are quick, inquisitive, and very attached to their mothers. These small bears play with Mom, their brothers and sisters, and by themselves. A stick, a flower, or their mother's ears are all toys to bat and chew.

Yearlings are a little more aggressive. Along with lots of mouthing and biting, they push, wrestle, and chase each other in short bursts. There seem to be lessons in what happens when you are overzealous in your behavior—one cub bites the other so hard that the bitten cub reacts in a way that shuts down the playtime. "If you bite me hard, I'm going to bite you hard." Cubs learn their limits quickly if they want play to continue.

Yearling cubs have longer play sessions than spring cubs, though eating can take precedence; they'll often play after they've fed or nursed. As in the case of Mutt, Jeff, and their sister, it's almost always sibling with sibling. Sibs play and they play often. And, as I've described, mothers and cubs stick together, separate from— even avoiding—other families. Because of this maternal avoidance behavior—not hanging out with other bears—cubs from different families seldom play with each other.

But mother bears can be playful, too, when playing with their own cubs. At four hundred to five hundred pounds, she dwarfs them, and I doubt the cubs could inflict any damage to her thick hide, but I'll often see a mother push away her cubs as they climb and bite.

Mothers and cubs play in muskeg swamps or open tundra good distances away from salmon streams. They seem to prefer spots with good visibility where they can see other bears approaching and where stressful situations are unlikely to unfold, like the one Poncho and Lefty picked for the play bout John and I photographed.

As they grow older, subadult bears are remarkably sociable. They are often found in close proximity to each other and frequently play together. The importance of this sociability is not understood, but the lack of aggression shown by these subadults to each other is conspicuous by its absence. When a bond still exists, a sib's favorite play partner is likely to be another sib. When the bond wanes, or as the bears mature, play with other bears increases.

So, Mutt is more likely to play with Jeff than with Fido, another same sized subadult who has a different mother. However, if the opportunity presents itself, especially if Mutt and Jeff aren't together, Mutt will play—even seek out and approach—Fido.

Frequently, I'll find several or more subadults in a sedge flat or around a fishing site. Chasing and short periods of play take place constantly. On the days when I sat amid these groups of bears, I often had a hard time keeping track of who was playing with whom.

Play continues as the bears grow older. Before the National Park Service increased the number that could be killed in the Katmai National Park Preserve, we used to watch groups of young male bears playing on the hillsides above Funnel and Moraine Creeks. Unfortunately, these young guys can become extremely tolerant of humans, and this makes them easy targets for bear hunters. At least in this heavily hunted area, the phenomena of four or five bears playing together has become a thing of the past.

To sum up my data collected over the years, more than half of the bears I have watched playing have been subadults. The majority of these subadult play bouts, close to 75 percent, were between males. About 20 percent were male-female, and less than 5 percent were female-female.

. . .

About every two weeks the Reverend Willis flew his Piper Super Cub the seventy miles from Egegik, where he lived, to our cabin at Becharof. His young daughter would throw our mail—carefully wrapped and attached to a roll of toilet paper complete with a streaming white tail (all the better to spot and find should the mail fall into heavy brush)—out the airplane window. Always accompanying letters from home were religious comic books featuring two soldiers named Holy Joe and Henderson. Holy Joe was the good guy and Henderson the sinner who finally sees the light. Obviously, the good reverend—and he truly was good in the best sense of the word—wanted to save our souls.

Forty years later Molly interviewed a woman for a job at her mental health agency in Homer. The woman said she was from Egegik, her maiden name was Willis, and her father was the reverend. Molly was amazed to learn the woman was the small girl who threw the mail out of the plane window.

We never knew that many people in Egegik thought we'd end up as red spots on the tundra thanks to hungry bears. And the Willises were not only kind enough to bring the mail the three years we stayed out there, but also, unbidden, to check on our well-being.

When we saw two subadult bears playing with each other and other subadults almost daily, of course we named them Holy Joe and Henderson.

People ask me how I take notes on bears at play all day. Well, the fact I love watching them makes it easy. When making observations of Holy Joe and Henderson as well as other bears, I'd set the stage by identifying the bears I thought might play and make my best guess of their age, size, and sex. I'd also record what they were doing—like fishing, grazing, resting, or walking. Once the bears made physical contact, I'd jot down what postures the play actually consisted of and how long it lasted. And when it ended and they started fishing or took off at a run, I'd write that down, too.

August 2, 1967

9 a.m. Lakeshore. 100 feet south of Cleo. Ongoing play.

HJ and H [Holy Joe and Henderson] on beach playing [when I noticed them]. Standing and pushing. HJ using teeth to hold onto H while shaking head. HJ pushing H over and grabbing H neck, H kicking up at him with back feet. Abrupt separation. Both ran over and into the creek, responding to splashing salmon? No sounds noted. Seven minutes O P [observation period].

August 14, 1967

10:30 a.m. Approx. 1 mile up on south side of Cleo.

HJ and H on hillside. Went to Site 3 [I had my most frequently used observation points numbered]. Bears both faced in our direction. Howie filming. HJ slid 20 feet down the hill on his back and shoulders then repeated. H sat. HJ did complete summersault almost standing on head [filmed]. Stopped and walked together down to the creek. 4 minute O P. H immediately caught salmon in riffles. HJ sat on bank then caught and completely ate large Dolly Varden trout.

This is the only time I've ever seen a bear sliding downhill, while almost standing on his head. He did it twice.

· · ·

To better understand the role of play, I also spent many hours documenting the other end of the behavioral continuum—potentially damaging fights and attacks, like those between two mature males or when a female is defending her cubs.

When bears fight they fight, when they play they play. There is not much middle ground. Watch two big males in a knock-down-drag-out with blood and hair flying, and then watch Poncho and Lefty rolling in the tundra gently nipping, licking, and nuzzling. You'll see the difference.

During fights bears don't bite with restraint like during play. Stiff-legged displays, foot twisting—literally rotating of feet in soft vegetation—head-down circling, and standing and rubbing against objects are all behaviors associated with potential damaging interactions. Add to this vocalizations—growling, huffing, and jaw popping—all sounds associated with aggression.

At times motivation for fighting seems obvious—competition for an estrus female, predation, food, a pesky subadult getting too close, or a place in the hierarchy—but without a way to measure physiological change during these encounters, I can't know how stressful these fights are for the bears involved. Bears are built to take it. While they have lots of big teeth, they also have thick skin, iron muscles, and heavy bones.

Even though I've seen dozens of them, watching a fight between big males is still brutal. Most of these altercations happen during spring mating season. On an early July day on the bottom part of Tutuk Creek, I was watching a large battle-scarred male fish for red salmon. A mature female appeared. I'd seen her breeding the day before, so I knew she was in estrus. Apparently, the male didn't see her, wasn't interested, or maybe was intent on catching the quickly moving fish. Whatever—he apparently didn't notice Jackson, that summer's alpha bear all other males had been deferring to, closely following the female.

In a flash Jackson grabbed the fishing bear by the back of the neck with a powerful bite, coming in from above and behind. The bear never had a chance to turn and in a split second he was on his back in the creek with the alpha bear tearing off pieces of hide. The unsuspecting bear managed to get to his feet, turn, and face his attacker, blood streaming from half a dozen wounds.

He stood stock-still and motionless, his only visible communication with Jackson was that he made no movement at all. Jackson faced him with head lowered and a river of drool extending from his mouth to the ground. Then Jackson backed away a few steps, turned, and broke into a run, hot on the trail of the female who hadn't stayed to watch the show. The beaten bear stood for a full minute, very gingerly left the creek, and was soon out of my sight.

Obviously, this was not play.

I have never seen one mature male kill another, although other people have. It must be incredible and sad. One mating season I did see two males in the proximity of an estrus female in a serious altercation. Instead of posturing, followed by brief contact and a few bites, the bigger of the two bears got the other down on its back in a savage attack. After ten or fifteen seconds of biting, he'd back off. As soon as the downed bear tried to get up, he'd move in again and chew some more. Hair was literally flying. The larger bear resumed this attack three or four times, then moved off looking for the female who had not stayed around to watch. The loser stayed on the ground and I was pretty sure he was mortally wounded, but after a few minutes he got slowly up and, with what certainly looked like great difficulty, walked away.

It's not easy to see blood on the coat of a dark-colored bear. I couldn't see any gushing out but could notice bleeding on his face and a large meaty tear on his neck. I never saw either of these two bears the rest of that summer.

Several times I've found the skull and parts of the skeletons of large male bears. Molly found one near the mouth of Mikfik Creek at McNeil. What happened to these bears? Slow-acting but eventually fatal wounds caused by errant shots from poor-shooting hunters could be one cause; however, after watching this fight between the two bears, I have little doubt murder does happen.

• • •

Today I still watch and record what I see—approach, head swinging, nuzzle, paw to head, mouth to ear, push, knock down, neck tug, wrestle, run, five-minute duration, sex, size . . . I continue to learn about how bears play in my quest to understand why.

Molly and my mother often talked to me about the importance of play in the development of an individual's capacity to have a healthy relationship, one filled with curiosity, creativity, and trust. Perhaps my mother's beliefs came from her friend Erik Erikson, certainly Molly's came from twenty-five years as a therapist. She also followed the teaching of D. W. Winnicott, a twentieth-century pediatrician and psychoanalyst who described play as "a basic form of living." Molly believes the development of self is creatively influenced by interaction with another person—and play helps us to build a sense of who we are and how we fit in the world.

I certainly won't compare bears and men using psychoanalytic

theory; however, I firmly believe play falls outside the normal survival tasks that both bears and humans typically engage in.

I remember John Morrow calmly laughing as we watched the antics
of Poncho and Lefty only a few feet away, and I think, perhaps—and
very unscientifically—that through play bears develop the kind of
trust that drives the behavior of man and beast alike.

# FIVE

## WATCH THE BEAR

**23**

# Alaska Bear Quest

A bear is a big, present, intelligent, charismatic animal—no more no less. They frighten and captivate. They certainly can and do hurt people, but almost always it is people who have done something, albeit inadvertently, to create the problem. Bears just want to go about the business of being bears.

I would have liked to think that there were bears that "loved" me, but I don't believe that was the case. They were interested, and because I tried to be predictable and nonthreatening, they spent time around me. After all, we have to be as entertaining to the bears as they are to us.

—Chris Day, bear guide

I've changed from being the kid who sat confused in front of blackboards of total gibberish in chemistry and math class, or when forced to define words I couldn't spell in English. Now instead of racing in the streets, skipping school, saddling up my horse, or picking up my shotgun, I've learned to go out in what's left of the wild and view a world with infinite questions to ponder. Maybe escape is what I've always done and chasing bears is just the latest episode. All I know is I'm happy when I do it.

• • •

I started my own bear-viewing company in 2001, naming it Alaska Bear Quest. Since then I've led hundreds of individuals, nature photographers, and film crews to see bears. These years have been some of the most rewarding of my life. The many seasons in the field have given me an opportunity to view bears in different habitats and sit-

uations. I've had my scientific theories on social behavior, communication, and play reaffirmed time after time.

Becoming a wildlife guide and making a few dollars has allowed
me to live the life I've always wanted. Of course, sometimes I have
to take people along with me on my trips, but I still get a high when
I step out of an airplane or boat onto a distant Alaskan shore. That's
what it's all about. The rest is just waiting to get out there.

I've spent time on rivers and bays along Shelikof Strait with magical names like Amalik, Kaflia, Kukak, Hallo, Sukoi, and Swikshak. I
watched bears at the mouth of the Kamishak River, on the banks of
Tutuk Creek, and camped and watched bears in the sedges at Chi-
nitna and Tuxedni Bays. When Bristol Bay red salmon enter their
natal streams on the western slopes of the Aleutian Mountains in
the Katmai National Park Preserve, I've spent days and weeks in
the winds and rain along Moraine and Funnel Creeks and Mirror
and Spectacle Lakes.

I've met people dedicated to wildlife conservation and had the
chance to fly and become friends with Alaska's best bush pilots.
Most importantly, I've had the opportunity to teach people about
bears and the places they live. And I think this is essential for the
long-term conservation of the species.

• • •

I've always liked hanging out with women and they've changed the
way I think. There were my mother's hunting stories and her interest in play, Molly's behavioral wisdom and love of animals, Sykes
Equine's thoughts and pets, and, for the past twenty years, the insights
of Chris Day.

Chris is small, slight, blond-haired, and attractive. She's also smart,
friendly, kind, well-mannered, and fearless. She has at least two college degrees. When she had her bear-viewing business, she could
meet ten clients at 8 a.m. and know everyone's name by 8:03. She
never complains or says she's cold. She can walk for miles in rubber hip boots and has a quarter horse mare named Reba that is at
least ten times bigger than she is. Reba in her five years of life has
never had a bit in her mouth and, while not being able to stand on
her head or talk, will do everything Chris asks of her.

I first met Chris in 1992 when she visited McNeil River. She had just arrived in Alaska from Wyoming and wanted to see brown bears. We watched them together for five days. I was immediately impressed with her knowledge of animals, her questions, and her calm demeanor around the bears we saw.

She credits me with teaching her a few things during her visit to McNeil, maybe, but during our first conversation I realized she was special and had an inherent sense of the minds and emotions of animals. Eventually I was to learn more from Chris than I ever taught her.

Sure, she was as awestruck as other visitors at the spectacle of McNeil, but as we stood on the viewing platform and looked out over the river and bears, her first observations were about the way the bears moved through their world and the fact that so much was going on we don't realize.

Chris lives a half mile away and she and Reba often stop by to visit Molly and me. While our talk is usually about gardening, children, and horses, it often turns to bears and the people involved with them—winter gossip in bear country. Naturally, no one ever knows or cares about bears as much as we do. Molly cuts people slack and tends to see a bright side for everyone. Not so, Chris and I—we like to label people as to whether or not they are scared of bears. In our book you are or you aren't. There is no middle ground. All too often we have seen people who say they aren't afraid quickly change when a bear approaches, moving rapidly back or reaching for their bear spray or shotgun.

Chris says that she has never been uncomfortable around bears. In her opinion, "They are no different to be around than any animal—horses, cattle, etcetera. You don't crowd them and don't let them crowd you. Have respect and be predictable."

Chris summed it up to a know-it-all "bear expert" who was pontificating on how to behave safely in bear country, "They're just critters, try treating them that way."

Like me, Chris has had her share of adventures. On that first visit to McNeil, she went for a beach walk by herself south of camp toward McNeil Head. She hadn't gone far when she saw a young bear feeding in the tidal flats maybe a quarter mile off shore. She climbed up on big flat rock—I've sat on the same rock—in order to see better, but as the tide came in toward the beach, so did the bear.

"The bear began walking in—he looked right at me and walked straight toward me, climbed up on the big flat rock, looked at me, huffed, and hopped on his front legs, then turned and climbed down and walked off. I looked right into that bears eyes and I'm not sure what I saw—eternity, god-something that made me feel very insignificant. I never felt threatened though."

Later Chris took the same beach walk, went to the same rock, and realized it was at the bottom of a bear trail that lead up through bluffs to the high country beyond. The bear was going to the trail and minding his own business when he noticed Chris hovering above where he wanted to go and became frightened, so he displayed at her. Chris had made "a rookie mistake" as she later told me, and realized she shouldn't have sat where she did.

Soon after visiting McNeil, Chris took a job managing a small "fly-in" bear-viewing lodge just north of McNeil. Soon thereafter she married the lodge's pilot, Ken Day, and since then they've lived happily ever after. However, before this big event—getting hitched to Ken—Chris had an unforgettable and amazing bear encounter.

One day, again walking by herself close to where the bears came daily to fish, she had a big mature male get up from where he was sitting and lumber in her direction. She knew the bear was used to being around people, as she saw him every day, and didn't think much of his approach until she realized he was coming directly toward her and not slackening his pace. She'd never had something like this happen before. There was nowhere to go, no rocks or trees to climb, all she could do is stand there. Chris later wrote in her journal:

When he got really close, I just talked with him—saying silly things like "I know you're not going to hurt me" . . . "you sure are pretty," etc.—well he walked right up to me—sniffed at me and proceeded to root into my belly 4 times—I had to brace myself to keep from being knocked off balance—I even then didn't feel threatened— well he turned walked about 3 steps, looked back at me, then walked a few more, stopped and looked at me again and then walked off.

So, as I said, my "intellectual" response was this bear isn't going to hurt me. Well, I can tell you my "instinctual" response was very different! When I was sure he was really walking away, my knees turned to jelly, I could hardly breathe.

From her first contact with bears, Chris instinctively knew how to act and fit in, never interfering in their lives or activities. She is also braver than guides and hunters who hide behind their large caliber weapons and resolutely defend their beliefs about the savagery of bears. She doesn't carry a bear deterrent. No guns, bear spray, or handheld flares—only a knowledge of bears and good judgment, which are the best deterrents of all.

Ken and Chris started Emerald Air Service and Day Trips in 1995. They pioneered the idea of single daylong trips across Cook Inlet from Homer. Using a single-engine de Havilland Otter that could land in rivers, lakes, and bays, they began taking people out from mid-May until bear-hunting season began in October.

Chris was without peer as a bear guide. Ken was pretty good, too, but flying ten people through the often-treacherous weather of Lower Cook Inlet, Shelikof Strait, and the Alaska Peninsula was a job unto itself. However, when he did guide, he wasn't exactly diplomatic in his remarks about clients staying together in a group or keeping quiet and being respectful around bears.

Ken is a pilot's pilot and among the best I've ever flown with. Like Chris he is a fierce defender of the rights of brown bears, doesn't suffer fools, and is a stern advocate for proper human behavior toward bears and vice versa. He hails from the mountains of Idaho, has a full beard and reddish-blond hair, and looks a bit like a brown bear. If you were in a bar feeling belligerent, you wouldn't pick on Ken.

As a couple, they taught people about the importance of protection and respect. They truly cared about the welfare of bears. This concern is what separated them from other viewing businesses who quickly copied their organizational skills and then followed them to the best viewing sites.

Today more than a dozen viewing companies thrive in Homer, plus more flying out of Kodiak, Soldotna, and Anchorage. There are boats taking out tourists as well as lodges that offer bear viewing to their guests. One Homer company has five planes and offers half-day trips; another has two aircraft and takes out twenty people at a time. Once it was determined the bears weren't the bloodthirsty creatures portrayed by the hunting industry, the race to make money was on. And make money, they have. A recent study from the University of Alaska found bear viewing in south-central Alaska brought in more than forty million dollars annually in direct sales. It is safe to say today bear viewing generates far more money than bear hunting, with the added benefit no bears have to die.

Fifteen years ago you could fly down Shelikof Strait and have a bay and thirty bears to yourself and your clients. Today the popular spots have five or six airplanes in the water or on the beach along with the roar of constant takeoffs, plus tour boats anchored off shore. Fifty people watching bears at one time is the new norm. I've seen mothers with cubs completely surrounded by three or four groups of tourists. I gave up visiting these places years ago. Who wants to witness a photographer perched on top of a dead whale taking pictures as big males arrive to feed? Or see a guy in wet suit surfacing in the middle of a gathering of bears who were trying to catch salmon. I cringed when I watched another fool crawl through high grass to "sneak" up on and get to within a few feet of a mother with spring cubs. I can't stand to see this disrespect for wildlife.

Ken and Chris started their bear-viewing business when I was still working at the McNeil Sanctuary. When I quit McNeil in 2000, I guided a few trips for them, and then I started my own business, Alaska Bear Quest, working with my friend Jon Berryman and Beluga Lake Air Service. Jon did the flying and I led the people. As well as doing day trips, I specialized in film crews and professional photographers who wanted to go out on multiday trips.

Ken, Chris, and I all treated the bears the same way by being predictable, keeping our groups small, and staying on trails we established where the bears expected us, and we always considered ourselves respectful visitors in their country.

• • •

One rainy day Chris and I had two bear-watching groups in a large estuary off Shelikof Strait. We kept a mile apart so as not to overwhelm our quarry and to maximize the experience of our clients. Five o'clock came and it was time to head for the floatplanes, which were parked near a beach some distance away. My group and I sat for a few minutes more than Chris's, continuing to enjoy a mother and two cubs of the year who were grazing in front of us as we sat quietly on a rock pile left by some long-forgotten glacier. Not wanting to disturb us and "our" bears, Chris led her group off the trail we normally used and out into the always-slick mud flats in the tidal area, now made worse than usual by the steadily falling rain.

As her group of nine carefully herded, slipping and sliding as they followed her, two subadult bears decided to make a running approach from several hundred yards away. Chris saw them coming and stopped, gathering her flock in a tight group behind her. Most of the time bears will stop some distance away, look you over, go on their way, and you can then continue your travels.

Not so these two, they kept right on coming at a gallop with mud splattering and water spraying. At about thirty feet they finally slammed on the brakes, perhaps not realizing they would not be able to immediately stop on the slick muddy surface, and both went into long skidding slides, finally coming to a halt less than fifteen feet from Chris. She reacted by putting up her arm and saying something I couldn't hear. Whatever it was made the bears turn around, and with great difficulty, slobber, and flying mud, they got their collective eight feet under them and ran away faster than they had come.

Some hours later back in Homer she said, "You know, there for a moment I wasn't exactly sure what they were up to."

It was no doubt very exciting for her clients as six hundred pounds of brown bear came barreling toward them with only a five-foot-tall, unarmed blonde separating them from eternity.

In 2013 Ken and Chris sold their successful bear-viewing business along with their beloved Otter. Viewing areas with lots of bears and good access had become overcrowded and many guides were obviously in it just for the money and not for the bears.

In 2015, a couple of years after Ken and Chris retired, I, too, stopped doing day trips but chose instead to work only on films for television.

We left a void to fill for people who wanted to see bears that were treated ethically, who wanted go to the best places and actually learn something about their quarry.

Dave Bachrach has always been interested in bears and cared about their welfare. But he has a far different background than Chris, Ken, or I do. Somewhere along the line, he sold a successful software company in California, met the famous bear man Charles Jonkel in Montana, read all he could about the Craigheads, and drove north to Alaska.

When he got to the "end of road," which is Homer, he went out on a bear trip with Chris and immediately felt he was in the right place and this would be his home. A few weeks later, after another trip with Ken and Chris, he decided he wanted to get into commercial bear viewing and "have an opportunity to teach and educate people and make a living at the same time."

He asked Chris for advice. "I wanted to jump-start the process so as not to make mistakes." Of course, Chris being Chris, she helped him out.

Then Dave had even more luck. There was conflict over the ownership of the lodge near McNeil River, the same one Chris had managed, and it sat empty. Not wanting it vandalized, the owners hired Dave as a "lodge sitter." For three months, except for my visits to the nearby salmon stream, he had the place and bears to himself.

Then a bear named Bob appeared on the scene, fully grown and much at ease around people. He was a new bear to me and of course to Dave. Bob's name came from his large scar. "Bite on butt" became "Bob." At first, he didn't do anything special except sometimes choose to sit close to Dave.

Dave had his first interaction with Bob when one evening he leaned a small outboard motor up against his skiff instead of securing it in place. The next morning the motor was lying in the sand thirty feet away surrounded by very large footprints. "You could see where the motor had been picked up then dragged," Dave described. As Bob was the only big bear around, Dave suspected he was the culprit.

He bolted the motor on to the boat, but a day later he could see deep tooth marks in the engine cowling. This time there was no doubt who the bad bear was, because Bob, evidently feeling no guilt, was resting a short distance away. As Dave watched, Bob got up from his nap, walked over to the boat, and removed two life jackets and an air horn. He bit into the life jackets and then started to gnaw on the air horn. Dave, fearing he might start chewing on the wooden boat next, decided to see if walking toward Bob might cause him to find something else to do. It worked; Bob moved away from the boat and dropped the air horn, but then in possible retaliation climbed the stairs of the deck attached to the lodge and proceeded to chew and destroy at least a dozen rubber crab buoys collected over the years by the lodge owners. Dave didn't care about the buoys so he left Bob to have a good time.

On several occasions Bob came up and looked Dave over as he sat alone, a few times sitting down a short distance away. When the two did meet on the big bear trail between the lodge and where the bears fished, Dave would step aside and Bob would walk on by.

Dave had lots of adventures and interactions with bears that can only happen if you are by yourself. He tells of the massive male that came up to him as he sat by himself next to the creek. The big bear appeared out of nowhere, walking into the area from somewhere upstream. The half-dozen bears who had been fishing quickly left the area. Apparently noting Dave, he gave him a sideways, "what are you doing?" look. The bear then proceeded to walk behind Dave, passing about ten feet away.

The next day Dave decided to take a break and sit on the bluff above the creek away from all the bear traffic on the stream bank. He hadn't been there long when along came the big bear.

"I was sitting purposefully between two bear trails so there was really no reason for him to come over," he says. But come over the bear did, walking to within a few feet. All Dave could think to do is say, "Hey. I'm here."

The bear looked startled when he said it, again gave him the curious "what the heck?" look and walked down to the stream.

In telling me about the big bear, Dave remarked, "One thing I quickly noticed was when you are by yourself bears are a lot more curious." An understatement by a man who many would think could have become part of the nutrient cycle of Kamishak Bay.

I'd say Dave learned how to get along with bears during those three months living by himself. You don't sit by yourself in the midst of fifteen or twenty bears day after day and not learn something, if only that bears don't seem to spend much time eating people.

Whatever happened, Dave came out of the experience with an attitude toward bears that closely mirrors that of Ken, Chris, and me.

So, a bear named Bob and three months alone contemplating bears got Dave started on the right foot to creating and running an outstanding and ethical bear-viewing company.

## 24

## Ephraim River

On today's early June bear-viewing trip, my clients are the Scotts, a middle-aged couple from California and their two grown children. When they booked the trip the previous winter, they said they'd been waiting for years for an opportunity to see brown bears. Now as we meet for the first time at the float-plane base in Homer, I size them up as agreeable and in reasonably good shape. It seems like a minor point but I always tailor my day around the physical ability of the clients.

I soon find they are intelligent people who want to learn everything there is to know about bears and Alaska. Enthusiastic, they packed all the gear I have suggested for our day—warm clothes, raincoats, plenty of food and snacks—they're ready to go. Standing next to the airplane, I give my brief talk on safety in bear country and how I would like them to behave on the trip.

"We're going to stick close together, walk single file, move slowly and talk quietly if a bear comes near. The bears may not be what you think or have been told," I said. "They are not apt to be aggressive; rather they can be quite timid. Quick movements, the sound of Velcro being quickly opened, or getting a raincoat out of a pack when a bear is approaching can scare a bear."

The father nods his understanding.

I also give them the information that when you go bear watching with me you only see male and female bears, and that I don't use, as many people do, the term "boar" or "sow," as these names are commonly associated with pigs. I could add, but don't, that I really like pigs—I've even raised a few—and have no intention of demeaning them, but bears and pigs are not even slightly related as some people believe. I add that pigs are classified in the scientific order Artiodactyla, along with deer, goats, sheep, and giraffes—they eat vegetation and have hooves. Brown bears are in the order Carnivora—they are omnivores with paws.

I always end the speech with a request:

> Please let me take care of the bears. It's my job. I've been doing this for a long time and I've never had a situation the bears and I couldn't handle. If I think a bear is getting a little pushy, I'll let the bear know. Let me be the one to decide how close we'll approach. Don't be surprised if I decide to walk away from a bear if I think it has had enough people for one day.

I make eye contact with each of the four for acknowledgment, to make certain everyone understands. This is serious business to me. Clients stay for only a short time before returning home to wherever they came from. The bears live where they do and, except for me, have to put up with brand new people almost daily. I want them to go about enjoying their lives as if I weren't there. To have this happen I have to be predictable in my behavior and ask my clients to do the same.

I'm amazed by how quickly people habituate to bears. I doubt this family will be any different. My clients often start a bear-watching trip with a "bears may eat me" belief, but after actually meeting a few realize this likely isn't true.

Departing on an early June morning from Homer, we fly south a hundred miles in a floatplane across Lower Cook Inlet to Ephraim River. We land in a quiet bay near the river's mouth. We pull our hip boots up and climb down the short ladder onto the plane's float, sit down, and carefully slide off into two feet of water. It makes for a very long and cold day of bear viewing if you are soaked at the onset. Together we wade the short distance into what is known as Silver Beach.

Jon, my good friend and the pilot, waits until we are safely ashore and then makes his daily ritual of leaving. He waves, starts the engine, turns into the wind, and takes off, disappearing into the distance. He'll return in eight hours.

We walk a few hundred yards and climb a sand dune where we can look out over a sedge grass meadow that extends two miles inland. We count at least thirty brown bears.

Silver Beach fronts a spectacular landscape—six miles of white sand backed by piles of driftwood tossed by waves up against sixty-foot dunes like the one we climbed. To the south, away from the sea, the dunes give way to lush green tidal areas and small streams. Back a few miles are mountains rising several thousand feet from the coastal plain.

Lying about ten miles from Silver Beach are the crown jewels of the Ephraim River country, Mount Douglas and Four Peaks Volcano. Rising from sea level, each reaches a height of seven thousand feet. Both of these dormant volcanoes are sheathed in glaciers and take up most of the eastern viewscape.

I have been to the Ephraim River estuary many times during the past twenty years. I know the trails, the best creek crossings, and where the tide will flood as it makes its way inland every twelve hours. The tide carries nutrients from the sea, which nourish the plants, which feed the bears, which creates the concentration of bears we are witnessing.

The Scotts are obviously delighted with the scene and, judging from their comments, wondering what will happen when we descend into what looks like a herd of wild brown bears.

"I count thirty-two bears. Is that fairly common?"

"We're going down there?"

"How close will we get?"

"Are we safe?"

"Are they all brown bears?"

I smile and do my best to set everyone at ease and answer as many questions as I can. I lead the family along a low ridge that parallels and extends the entire length of the meadow. The ridge is actually the top of an old sandy beach berm, once shoreline but now inland half a mile from the ocean. Over time the land we are walking on has risen, freed from the incredible weight of the not-so-distant glaciers as they melted, and receded inland.

We are walking on a heavily used bear trail. In places it is a distinct double track, two narrow paths separated by three or four inches of vegetation. Some stretches are worn away by the big feet of traveling bears, leaving only a single wide pathway, a comfortable walking width for both humans and bears.

Because I want my clients to learn as much as they can about bears, we stop and I explain what we are seeing.

"At least some bears have the behavior of walking in each other's footprints, literally placing their feet exactly where a previous bear has walked," I say. "They undoubtedly also leave information on the grassy strip in the center of the trails as well as in each other's footprints, likely leaving individual scent markers, as they move along."

I add, "Bears use time as well as space to separate themselves from bears they don't wish to meet or socialize with—mothers with cubs steer clear of large males, young bears tend to avoid intolerant females. Scents on the trail tell bears exactly who has been there and when they passed."

I give my clients this information and they appear politely attentive but maybe getting a little bored. Here's some guy talking about bear trails and Latin names, and right out there are the live bears we came to see. They perk up when I finish my discourse with the old adage describing the olfactory capabilities of a bear: "Our nose is to a dog's nose as a dog's nose is to a bear's."

We continue on. Most of the more than thirty bears we had seen when we started are still a quarter of a mile away. I point out fresh bear droppings and bits and pieces of angelica, a plant high in protein and a June favorite of brown bears. Scattered on this sandy ridge are shallow depressions bears have dug over the years. These "bear beds" overlook the sedge flat.

I point out that these spots offer a place to rest as well as give the occupant a chance to see other bears before they come too close. Some of these beds are two or three feet deep and six or seven feet across.

I tell the Scotts a well-meaning national park ranger told me at great length these "belly pits" were dug by bears whose stomachs had gotten big in the fall after a summer of feasting on salmon and they were uncomfortable lying on flat ground. He said they dug these depressions to make room for their rounded bellies, hence the term "belly pits." Some Park Service ranger information serves the public; some just keeps old wives' tales alive.

The truth of the matter is bears dig these pits or beds in spring and fall when they may be skinny or fat. I know from my years of observation that smaller and presumably younger bears as well as mothers and cubs all use the hillside beds. They like to rest in a location where they can see other bears coming and where a bear can escape the almost ever-present coastal wind. Conspicuously absent users of this string of bear beds are large males who plop down pretty much where they want, apparently not caring who comes walking up on them or how hard the wind blows.

As we look at and contemplate the bears in the distance, there is sudden movement in the alders not more than fifty feet from where we are standing. Alders sway, branches snap and a female bear appears. Moving quickly, she cuts diagonally across our trail. All four Scotts crowd together. No one gets between the bear and me. I'm pretty sure I know what's coming next and sure enough, in less than a minute, a big male bursts out of the brush on the female's trail. We are most likely seeing an estrus female being pursued by a suitor.

Nice-looking mature female, I say to myself. Blond color, well furred, her winter coat still intact. I estimate her to weigh about five hundred pounds. He's a handsome dark male, at least twice as large as she is, with a few wet alder leaves stuck on his face, which makes him look a little silly.

He stops for a moment and faces our way, slobber and drool adding to his tense facial expression, and then he quickly turns and gallops off after the female. No one is hurt or eaten. The family of four doesn't say a word, as they stare silently at the spot where the bear—a beast almost five feet tall at the shoulder—has just stopped and looked them over. There is nothing like a big salivating brown bear at close range to focus your attention.

As always, I answer as best I can as the tenor of the questions changes: "How big was he? How much did he weigh? How old do you think he was? What if he had charged us? What would you have done?"

I'm ready.

"I've never had a problem in a situation like this one," I say. "The bear had room to look us over. Staying together in a group was the proper thing to do. The truth of the matter is bears don't really have the aggressive behavior most people credit them with."

I want to get moving, we have miles to go and bears to see.

• • •

We head for the far end of the meadow and a group of four bears that have been feeding in a small area for the past three days. As I visit this place almost daily I am able to keep track of a few easily identifiable bears. Mating season is in full swing, and we can see bears that are actually coupled as well as males following females—like the two we just saw. We also spot a few immature or subadults, as bears three or four years old are sometimes called, and fair number of young males, breeding-age bears not yet fully grown. Present, too, are recently weaned two-and-a-half-year-old bears. Their mothers, now in estrus, are some of the females being chased by the big males.

Everyone wants to see females with cubs, and my bear-viewing clients are no different. They keep asking and I keep looking. Finally, at the very edge of the meadow almost a mile away, I spot a mother with three big cubs. As we watch they walk out of the sedges and disappear into the dense alder and willow. I cross my fingers and hope they'll come back.

Few bear families frequent this particular meadow at this time of year. For the most part (I never say "never" when talking about bears) these bears, particularly females with newborns, come down from the hills later in the spring, seemingly preferring to stay away from sedge flats and concentrations of amorous and sometimes predatory big males.

The Scotts and I wait for a few minutes to see if the mother and cubs return. She keeps out of sight so I start toward the group of four bears I'd spotted in the distance that I hope will be the highlight of everyone's day.

As we walk I explain I have been watching these particular bears for more than a week and I don't understand everything I've seen. It's a completely atypical group. In fact in the past fifty years I've never seen anything like it, four bears of different sizes, sexes, and presumably age interacting together is far from common. I give them a quick run-down on brown bear social behavior and which bears are likely to be together. I think the family is listening; it's a little difficult to tell as they are walking behind me.

Right now, my plan is to move off the ridge we are on, descend to the meadow where the four bears are feeding and sit on a driftwood log and keep movement and conversation to a minimum. I want my clients to appreciate this extraordinary group and also have the opportunity to watch and experience bears as individuals.

The biggest bear in the group of four is a very large dark brown male. I'd guess he weighs more than a thousand pounds. He is huge, as big as any bear in the meadow, and based on body size and the innumerable scars lacing his head, neck and shoulders, he is mature—at least ten or twelve years old. Large males are apt to be scarred, almost assuredly from fights over estrus females or for a place in the hierarchy. Occasionally females defending their cubs might bite and claw them. This particular male had half of his right ear missing, not an uncommon occurrence, as bears sometimes reef on each other's ears during encounters. There are no handholds on a bear.

The four bears graze continuously, reminding me of a bucolic childhood scene on our farm. I explain that large males, like the one now in front of us, typically keep to themselves. Sometimes however, and it's quite spectacular when they do, they play with other bears of the same size and sex. These play sessions usually occur when they are full of fish or happen upon what could be an old chum or even possibly a littermate in the right mood.

I tell the Scotts I've learned over the years there seems to be a strong correlation between the availability of food and the degree of sociability bears exhibit toward each other. Now, even though food is plentiful, there is aggressive competition for estrus females, and most big males aren't in playful moods.

Two of the bears in the group are young males, nearly as tall as the large male but with much lighter and lankier bodies. I'd named them Willie and Waylon as much for the entertainment of my guests as for myself. If they were humans, I'd describe them as being in their late teens. Mature males bulk up with muscle, as they grow older. Young adults like these two put their energy into skeletal growth. The two bears had been playing together all week. Occasionally, they played with the big male. They appeared to do this gently, likely not want-ing to elicit an unwanted response from the far larger bear.

We turn our attention to the bear closest to us. I tell my captive audience she's a small female and I don't know if she is a subadult or a sexually mature bear. In the week I've been watching her, I never saw her mating, but my observation begs a question: Could she have gone in and out of estrus prior to my being on the scene? Maybe. Females for the most part first mate somewhere between four and seven years of age. Based on her size and behavior I'd take a wild guess and say she was a three- or four-year-old and weighed two hundred fifty to three hundred pounds. She looked about quarter the size of the large male and less than half the size of the two young males.

It was a very unusual group of bears, not only in size, sex, and age but also in that each one at one time or another played, greeted, or at least touched all the others.

One frustrating and important thing about watching wildlife is that you never know what happened before you got there. The female could have been mating with any or all of her companions in the weeks before I began to observe them—she could have been far older than I thought. Or she could have just been a small bear. Usually if a female is sexually mature and has recently weaned her cubs, you'll spot her prominent nipples as brown bears nurse right up to sepa-rating from their cubs. But this particular female didn't seem to be one of these mother bears—she looked and acted young.

The two young males could have been her cubs from a previous litter—littermates often hang out together for at least several years after they are weaned—and have been known to stay in the same area and sometimes even follow their mothers around for a year or so.

These are the thoughts going through my mind as I watch this group. Here's what happens to me: I start watching bears, get into imagining their lives, bliss out, and become a bit of a space cadet. I long ago realized I wouldn't be able to identify every bear I saw or know their life histories. One thing I did know and could take com-fort in was that the bears knew who they were and I was the only confused one.

Back to reality, I decide to move a little closer. I lead my clients off the ridge and the bear trail to the edge of the meadow. We sit down on a convenient log about fifty yards from the feeding bears. I feel I've imparted enough knowledge for at least a little while and suggest we watch quietly.

After a few minutes, the female appears to be watching us as we watch her. She munches on sedge for a few seconds, then raises her head and glances in our direction. Bears tend to move slowly as they eat, sometimes pausing to sit or even lie down.

This bear had several options. She could feed away from us, or else feed in our direction. She also had the whole state of Alaska to move to, and acres of ripe sedges around her. In spite of these opportunities, she began to move our way.

I love to watch people as they watch bears. I turn slightly so I can see the Scott's faces. These folks don't miss a thing as the bear walked slowly toward them. As instructed, they sat as still and quiet as clams. I was pretty sure what was going to happen next, and I could have told them, but I hate to spoil any one's bear trip.

When the bear gets to within seventy-five feet my clients begin to glance at me; at fifty feet the father asks, very softly, "Isn't she getting a little close?"

I smiled reassuringly. At about twenty feet the bear stops, slowly sits down on her haunches, and simply looks at us all sitting in a row on our log. I hoped everyone remembered the speech about bear etiquette I gave before leaving Homer.

Everyone does and remains silent. Bears get mighty big when they come sit in front of you, even small ones like this female. You can see the swirling patterns of the hair on her face, the length of her nose, the whiteness of her teeth, the prominence of her ears, and the unfathomable and mysterious look coming from her small brown eyes. She watches us for a long minute then abruptly turns over on her back and raises all four feet in the air.

I peek at my clients—remember this bear is only twenty feet away. They are enthralled. The bear begins to place each paw in her mouth, licking her long claws. She grabs a convenient stick and holds it between her front paws while biting at it. After a few minutes of acrobatics, she heaves herself to her feet and walks to within about ten feet of our log. I know it was this close because every single client invariably measures the distance after the fact. I'm not watching the Scotts now because I'm giving the bear my full attention. Slowly I stand up, the bear stops, looks at me, turns, and walks back to her feeding friends.

My clients don't say a word for at least thirty seconds. When breathing resumes, they repeat to me exactly what I had just seen.

"She sure came close."

"I could hear her breathing. Was she trying to smell us?"

"What did she want?"

The general consensus was that this was about the coolest thing ever and the day was a complete success. However, as sometimes happens when bears are extremely close, no one remembered to take any pictures.

I shared with the group how Chris Day once forwarded me an email that told the story of a hunter on Alaska's North Slope who had a bear approach his camp only to turn over on its back with its feet in the air, playing with its paws just as our bear had done. His scared partner wanted to shoot, but reason prevailed and they took pictures instead.

She asked me what I thought had gone on, of course I had no way of knowing for sure, but imagined the bear came over to see the hunters for any number of reasons. They were something new, an oddity in the North Slope landscape. I teach in my college classes that it's to an animal's evolutionary advantage to explore its environment and that brown bears are one of the most successful terrestrial mammals in existence.

However, bears, like other animals, can get caught between conflicting motivational drives. When the bear approached perhaps this is what happened. Here was something new and novel and the bear was unsure whether to threaten or flee. Classical ethologists like myself believe that sometimes when this happens an animal may pick a third behavior—in this case play.

Chris thought perhaps the bear wanted to get close and check the hunters out, but did something it knew how to do which was to act submissive—to reassure the strangers that it meant no harm. As usual I think Chris was right.

We leave the four to their sedge eating and spent the next few hours watching and photographing bears mating, grazing, resting, chasing and playing, enjoying our day in the Alaska sunshine.

In late afternoon we turned back down toward the ocean where our plane would return for our scheduled pick up. Our path led back past the same four bears, but kept us on a ridge a good fifty feet above them. Normally, we don't stop on the way to the plane to watch bears, as they have a way of getting between you and your destination and making you late for scheduled pickups. I'd learned this lesson a few times in my early years. However, in the spirit of giving them the right of way—after all it's their place—you occasionally have to wait until they move along to wherever they're going.

Today I break the rules and stop for a moment—not wanting the warm summer day to end—and not realizing what the bears were going to do. As if on cue, they moved as a group up out of the meadow and right onto the trail between us and our pickup point. Walking around them, something I've done innumerable times, would have been difficult. The steep slope the bears had just climbed lay on one side and dense, hard to walk through alders on the other. I really could have gone in either direction, however this was a bear-watching trip, and here were the last bears of the day.

When it became apparent the bears were blocking our way, I told everyone we'd just have to wait to see what they had in mind. Tired from the miles of walking we'd logged, we all happily plopped down in the grass to wait our turn.

I have to smile at my clients' newfound ease. This morning they navigated a big bear at fifty feet, then a small female even closer. Now just eight hours later, they're relaxed enough to sit down and enjoy the approaching bears.

Angelica grows for about a mile in all directions so the bears have quite a bit of latitude in picking a feeding location. Perhaps they thought we were eating in an especially abundant and tasty spot. Whatever the reason, all four bears walked over to where we were sitting, separating as they grazed and ultimately surrounding us. No sign of aggression or any alarming behavior. However, they were apparently keeping track of us with frequent looks in our direction. At one point the little female wandered over and plunked down about twenty-five feet from us. The big male stayed farther away munching from plant to plant.

There's nowhere to go as we sat among the bears—no reason to move. It's one of those moments you couldn't orchestrate. Ten or fifteen minutes after it began it ended. As if they receive a collective signal, the bears stopped eating and, led by the small female, walked back down the hill to the tidal flat. We rose and continued our walk to the waiting airplane. No one spoke; we walked as silently as the bears had.

There's a story about a white oilfield guy visiting a village on the Arctic Ocean. He strikes up a conversation with an old man whose family had inhabited the area for at least ten thousand years. The white man, trying to impress the resident with his sophistication and great knowledge, spends half an hour describing man's first trip to the moon. The Yupik man, well known for his wisdom and mystical powers, listens politely until the man talks himself out, then says simply, "You know, I have been to the moon many times."

Why did the bears on our day at Ephraim River behave as they did? Why did they move toward us? Why not feed away? What was the reason for the unlikely makeup of the group? Why did they stay together?

We can endlessly speculate. But it was simply a moment on a beautiful spring day when man and beast sat down together.

Sometimes I feel like the Yupik man. I don't need to demystify the unknown, nor do I need culture and technology to watch and enjoy bears.

# 25

## Bear Watching

I once saw brown bears playing ice hockey in a Russian circus. Teaching a bear to walk on its hind legs, let alone getting it to wear skates, to hold a hockey stick, hit a puck—these would be difficult tasks.

Wild bears have a far better life than their captive brethren and don't have to play hockey or wear numbered shirts. But they, too, have to be able to do many difficult things in order to survive. It's observing what they do and how they do it that makes bear watching such a fascinating vocation.

One of my favorite spots to watch bears is the canyon at the top of Funnel Creek in Katmai National Park Preserve. Each summer thousands of red salmon move through here, on their way to spawning beds further upstream. During salmon season a half dozen bears or more can be seen actively fishing.

In most places on Funnel Creek, bears stand in the current facing downstream waiting for salmon to swim up to them. These salmon are fast, agile, and on the lookout for predators—the bears being the major one on this part of their journey. The salmon are far from easy for a bear to catch. In the canyon however, bears have figured out how to do it. Here they face upstream and wait for salmon to come downstream. Sounds complicated, but what's happening is after many miles of fighting their way against the current, the fish apparently tire and as a result sometimes stop for a few minutes, drifting back down to pools out of the current where they can rest before continuing their journey. Over eons and generations, the bears have learned food will come floating by. They patiently wait and grab.

Another time in another place, I saw an elderly female trying to catch a single salmon that had become trapped in a pool on a small stream. The salmon was intent on escaping downstream past the bear who was standing in the creek at the outlet of the pool. The fish would make a try, the bear would lunge and miss, and the salmon would turn and go back upstream to the relative safety of deep water. This went on three or four times, the salmon trying both sides of the bear as it stood in the water almost blocking the small creek. Each time the salmon moved, the bear would duck its head in the fish's direction. The salmon evidently seeing the movement would turn and retreat. On about the fifth try—and this is really true—the bear faked left, the salmon went right, and quicker than you can say bull-shit, the bear wheeled and nailed the fish to the bottom with a great paw. You don't see bear-fish interactions like this every day.

I realize that today my bear-watching stories are a lot more benign than they used to be. No more getting chased into the lake with Molly on my shoulders, waking sleeping bears with Howie, or getting hop-charged by Woofie. Both the bears and I seem to have settled down and I'd rather tell people about waiting with a photographer by a dense stand of purple lupine and being lucky enough to have Sol-stice and her cubs wander through for an unforgettable image. Or of later that same summer sitting for two hours by a field of pink fire-weed until another bear stopped to sit and pose.

Watching bears at the same places year after year is much like watching a soap opera, except with all the episodes and stories hap-pening at once. It's not difficult to identify with the actors and I keep returning so I won't miss anything. I want to know what hap-pens next. Did Julie have cubs? Has Solstice come back? Will Pon-cho finally become the top bear? Will it be a good berry year? How was the fish run?

I've got no plans to stop.

· · ·

Frequently, people call me and ask my advice before they go bear watching. I want them to have a good time, to be safe, to return with stories and pictures, but I also want to protect the bears from human invasions into their home. Sadly, many bear watchers go heavily armed, so I'm happy to tell people what I have learned with the hope they won't shoot a bear they've misunderstood.

There's no doubt bears are best left alone; however, with planning based on the behavior of the bears and regulations to keep people in line, it can be done safely and be minimally disruptive. Nevertheless, bears can be driven from specific localities by viewing pressure. They can also move their schedules to times when humans aren't present.

So, if you go bear watching, the two most important things you can take with you are a knowledge of bears and common sense. I stress the common sense. Long ago I took a ranger from the Adirondack Park out to watch bears. I asked him if he ever had any problems with people and black bears. I'll never forget his answer. "I've had a couple." Then he added, "And both times people had let bears into their cars."

If you have a bear or bears in sight, watch the bear. If you approach, make sure the bear is comfortable with you. When viewing bears, make absolutely certain you do not alter the activity the bears are engaged in—the bear is making a living—you're just an interloper and a soon to be gawker. It might help to think of yourself that way.

It is important to be completely predictable in your behavior, and be ready to stand your ground should a subadult or cub approach. A learning experience for you is a learning experience for these young bears. Your actions can easily influence the bear's future interactions with people.

I suggest finding a place to sit where the bear can easily see you, where it has ample opportunity to look you over from a distance. Pretend the bear is watching you and knows you are there, because you can bet that it does.

And I remind anyone who will listen to never surprise a bear. Period. As Chris Day says, "To do so is very rude, and you don't want to be rude to a bear." Surprising a bear will most likely end in unwanted results: the bear finding a different place to spend the day or telling you it is unhappy with your behavior.

As you go on your bear-watching adventure, remember bears just want to go about the business of being bears. It's a testament to their tolerance that more people don't have adverse encounters with them.

From the beginning I realized I'd be a disruptive influence on the lives of the bears I watched. I needed them. They sure as heck didn't need me. I sacrificed their peace and tranquility for my own gain—science, money, a life in the wild. I did it anyway.

Alaska is bear country. You can expect to meet a bear most anywhere. Obviously, where bears congregate is where you want to be. Most everyone wants to see mothers and cubs because they are so cute and cuddly and make for interesting pictures.

So why not go out and find a bear like Solstice? She's used to people and lets you get close. But I've never seen her before July and the onset of the first red salmon run at Tutuk Creek. She might be anywhere in the months before that. After all her home range could be ten to fifty square miles or more. Aside from around her den site—if you are lucky enough to find it—the best chance to see her would be in the sedges of a tidal estuary. But it could be she's on some river bar as she digs for the carcasses of last year's silver salmon. If the tides are right, she might be somewhere on the seashore clamming or maybe on a sunny mountainside eating some tasty early greens. Once in mid-June, flying over the Alaska Peninsula, we saw a very blond bear, almost assuredly her in an open meadow only a mile from Tutuk Creek.

Much as I'd like to see her in May and June, it's a very big country, so I wait for July to plan on visiting her. She tends to turn up when the salmon appear. In fact, for more than twenty years she has turned up at to Tutuk Creek with the first set of big tides in July. She generally stays for the entire month, rarely missing a day of fishing. When I watch her I only have two or three places where I sit. I like to think this is where she expects to see me. I want to be predictable. I never sit on the north side of the east-west running creek. I leave this entire area for her and other the bears where they are free to come and go without having to walk by me. Maybe the payoff is she keeps coming back, largely ignores me, and never minds when her cubs walk over to see how close they can get before I shoo them away.

Before I move down near the creek to get closer to the bears, I stand on the high stream bank and give any bears present the opportunity to look me over. I do not sneak down on them. I never hide. I do move slowly and try my best to keep my movements to a minimum.

Solstice eats hundreds of salmon during her month on the creek. But salmon runs are finite and the Tutuk run is usually over by the end of July. She leaves Tutuk Creek and goes somewhere else in August. If I knew the run timing—when the salmon leave the ocean for freshwater—of nearby streams I might be able to find her, but likely she's up at Tutuk Lake, walking along the lakeshore for any spawning salmon that have wandered into shallow waters.

September, Solstice again could be anywhere. She might have gone twenty miles west to feast on red salmon in Moraine Creek in the Katmai Preserve. I've never seen her there and neither has Dave or Chris, but we certainly don't see every bear. It's a huge area.

Come September and October silver salmon enter Tutuk Creek. Instead of going all the way to the lake like the red salmon of July, the silvers spawn in the creek and become prey to the bears. Typically, there are five or six bears fishing along the length of the creek plus one or two more at the outlet. Solstice could be one of these bears.

· · ·

There are rules and regulations in national parks to protect wildlife and habitat from visitors. I've long abided by them because much of my bear guiding was in Katmai and Lake Clark National Parks. I've obeyed the law, while knowing many regulations were wrong and all too often based on someone's bureaucratic imagination, total lack of field experience or scientific evidence.

Statewide, Alaska Department of Fish and Game employees are slowly getting over their "bearanoia." But old beliefs die hard—fearsome beast, worthy target. At McNeil I've observed Fish and Game staff evolve from using shotgun-fired firecracker shells, air horns, and rubber bullets to using rocks, hand claps, and finally gentle talking to remove bears from camp.

Each summer thousands of people safely watch bears up and down the coast of Alaska and British Columbia. It's a big business, bringing in millions of dollars into state, provincial, and local economies. But like bear hunting, it is an industry needing careful regulation. Many bear-watching companies put profit well ahead of the bears, bringing in tourists who don't really care about bears but who simply want to see one.

· · ·

Twenty years ago I was lucky enough to author a booklet titled *Living in Harmony with Bears*. Now out of print but still available on the internet, it contains suggestions for successful bear viewing.

Other titles I recommend: Dr. Stephen Herrero in *Bear Attacks: Their Causes and Avoidance* is a classic. Dr. Terry DeBruyn's *Walking with Bears* has by far the best information available on black bears. I only wish I had known Terry when he was following bears through the woods of Michigan. Dave Smith's *Backcountry Bears Basics: A Definitive Guide to Avoiding Unpleasant Encounters* is a wonderful and informative book. If you get to the part about "sex in the wild," you'll note I had some input.

All these books offer advice on how you should behave around bears but also stress the importance of knowing about bear evolution, biology, and behavior.

I speak a different language than many wildlife managers. I can remember how excited I was fifty years ago when I allowed bears to first come over to look at me. It took me a few seasons to overcome my fears, learn my tolerance levels, and recognize bears as individuals who were not the same creatures as characterized by bear hunters.

The bottom line on bears and bear watching is this: Don't let your or someone else's fear of bears ruin your enjoyment of the outdoors. Do it. Go. The statistics of surviving are greatly in your favor.

# 26

## Snow Bear

A few friends around Homer note when they first see bear tracks in the spring. They'll call and tell me where, as they know I'll be interested. Fresh bear tracks in the snow mean we've gotten through another winter.

The first bears to appear are usually black bears feeding on new green plants in snow-free sections of the bluffs along the south-facing shore of Kachemak Bay, east of Homer. Bears are often killed here as they eat. Their black, glossy coats are easy to spot against leafless vegetation and white snow patches.

Brown bears, for the most part, but certainly not always, den at higher elevations and emerge later than their smaller relatives. The first evidence of brown bears is apt to be the tracks of larger bears, presumably males, wandering around in the hills looking for mates, winter-killed animals, or moose caught in and unable to escape the still deep snow.

I live about fifteen miles from town, at a 1,250-foot elevation. We have three to four feet of snow on the ground for five or six months, even with global warming, while the sea-level town of Homer has very little continuous snow cover.

From time to time black bears den near our house and there is a known brown bear denning area about five miles away at an elevation of about 2,500 feet. This area was identified by ADF&G biologists after immobilizing and placing GPS devices on several bears. Late one April, not too long ago, I started making daily ski trips into the spot with the hope of observing some emerging bears.

I'm a devotee of "skate" skiing, which involves narrow skis and propelling forward with a skating motion. It's an Olympic event that takes place on wide, hard-packed trails groomed with special machines. In the spring when conditions are right, we have what must be the best skate skiing in the world. When the snow melts in the daytime then freezes at night, it leaves a hard crust. I can glide over snow-covered alders and creeks with little effort. My morning ski, before the crust melts and temperatures rise for the day, can easily be ten or fifteen miles.

One spring day out with my dog, I crossed the trail of a very large bear. I knew the tracks were fresh as they hadn't been there the previous morning. They crossed and recrossed a narrow valley and made me think the bear was looking for something. I kept my faithful Lab at heel in case we came unexpectedly on the bear.

After coming face to face with so many of them, I've overcome my fear of bears. But this day, as I follow its tracks over hard-packed snow, the unseen bear still felt formidable. Suddenly, it was just me and the bear out there in the great white. I had to remind myself it was the same old bear of summer. We followed the tracks for miles but never saw the bear.

When following bear tracks, one can go forward and backward as both directions tell a story of what the bear has been doing. Following bear tracks is one of my favorite pastimes.

Another time, on a miles-long muskeg swamp, some friends and I came over a rise to see a big, dark male "post-holing" through the snow crust, which supported our skis but not his great weight. We watched as he reached an open spring and drank for several minutes. I'm meditating on the thought that this might be his first drink in months, when my companions get a little loud in their questions to me: "Are we safe?" "Do you think he'll come up here?" "How big is he?" "Do you think we should move?"

I answered with my usual response to such inquiries: "Don't worry—they only eat women and children"—there were three women in our party.

The bear evidently heard the talking, turned, and took off at a run. He was still running and breaking through the crust when he disappeared over a ridge a mile away.

I once witnessed a mother black bear and her three small cubs at the mouth of their den. Tucked in an alder patch on the side of a steep ravine, the den would have been invisible if I hadn't been looking down on it. I left after a few minutes, not wanting to disturb her or cause her to leave the security of her winter home.

When I went back to look a few days later, I saw no sign of her but did see two subadult brown bears a few hundred yards from the black bear's den. I assumed, because I hadn't seen them or their tracks the day before, they had only recently emerged from their den. I watched for over an hour until they disappeared into some nearby timber. I waited for a few minutes and slowly followed their tracks but gave up when the going got difficult due to downed trees killed by a spruce bark beetle infestation. I skied back and had no trouble finding the den where they had spent the winter. I never did examine the inside, in case they wanted to return, something they didn't do during the next week.

I'd never seen a mother brown bear with spring cubs at their den site, so the next year I started looking for them in late April. My daily ski route took me along a low ridge, paralleling—across a narrow valley—the mountainside, which I knew to be used by bears. On May 15, from a distance of about two hundred yards, I saw what looked to be a muddy trail in the snow. I stopped and waited and to my utter amazement from out of a depression surrounded by low willows came a mother brown bear and her three small babies. Spring cubs! This was about as excited as I'd ever been when watching bears.

The family walked about fifty feet from the bottom of a dead spruce, stayed a few minutes, then turned and went back the way they'd come, once again disappearing. I moved to where I could see better and with the aid of a spotting scope was able to make out where snow had been disturbed and the bears' trail ended. With no visible path except the one to the tree, I felt she had returned to her den site.

The next day it snowed with accompanying poor visibility, so I stayed home. The day after, I went out but there was no sign of the bears, trails, or digging due to more than a foot of new snow. As I skied home—passing the last steep hillside on the small mountain the bears had denned on—I looked up and there at the base of a huge, forty-foot-high, windblown snowdrift were the bears. I kept on moving, again not wanting to disturb them, and didn't stop until I was a quarter of a mile away.

Apparently, she had dug a new den in the firm snow of the drift.

I came back the next day and she was still there. It would have been fun to go back and watch and ultimately follow; however, Homer is far from a wilderness, and coyotes and wolves make good targets for the many snow machines in the area. Bears, if not "taken" or killed, are often followed and harassed, and these bears didn't need me to advertise their presence. It may have been she had abandoned her den because of my being near, but perhaps, and as I like to think, her winter den had flooded due to snowmelt, and she had moved to a drier springtime abode.

These were each unforgettable sights of beautiful animals. I have yet more great memories. And each is one more bear story. Sadly, scenes like this are becoming rare around here. The state of Alaska has determined there are too many bears, so why not kill a few more? They decided hunting bears using bait is a worthwhile way to do this. Many bears have been killed as they feed at baits consisting of dog food and fish scraps not far from where the mother bear sat with her cubs that day.

# 27

## Sterling

The government trapper who took the grizzly knew he had made
Escudilla safe for cows. He did not know he had toppled the spire
off an edifice a-building since the morning stars sang together. . . .
Escudilla still hangs on the horizon, but when you see it you no
longer think of bears. It's only a mountain now.

—Aldo Leopold, *Sand County Almanac*

For many years I taught Bear Behavior and Conservation inside a classroom at our local branch of the University of Alaska. However, several summers, thanks to Ken and Chris Day and their airplane, I was able to go "hands-on" with real live bears and held continuing education classes for Kenai Peninsula teachers on a salmon stream in Lower Cook Inlet. I'd fly out a group of ten, make camp, and we'd watch bears for a week.

These were great trips. The teachers learned to tell males from females and cubs of the year from yearlings. They collected bear hair for DNA samples off rubbing posts we set up, and identified individual bears to see if we could determine if a linear hierarchy existed in our small study area. We'd cook and eat together and each evening I'd conduct a class going over everything we'd seen during the day.

The teachers were quick learners. As they watched fifteen to twenty different bears every day, those bears went from nondescript animals to individuals living in a complex social organization. Within an hour of arrival at our viewing spot, the students had bears identified and named. From there it was a short jump to make the discovery that Susie always deferred to Teddy, or that Jackson stopped fishing and departed the area when the far bigger Bruno arrived. While each group gave the bears new names, the bears never seemed to mind.

When the salmon entered the creek, a few people were appalled as the bears lunched on their catch with no apparent feelings for the fish. Quickly enough, the horrified comments were replaced with curious observations:

"He took a bite out of the head, do bears like brains?"

"He ate the skin first, why did he do that?"

"Was that a male or a female salmon?"

One day, after watching and learning about bears, the teachers and I were in the last half mile of a two-mile walk back up the stream valley to our camp. We walked closely and as usual I led the group, clapping my hands and uttering, "Hey bear, ho bear" when the visibility was poor, making sure we didn't startle any bears on the trail.

I heard a quiet voice from the back of the line ask, "Do you know there's a bear following us?"

No indication of panic, just a good student I had obviously taught well.

We'd spent the day with fishing bears wandering as close as twenty feet and I'd been reminding everyone: "If you have an encounter with a bear, don't escalate the situation. Let the bear call the shots. If he or she does something, then you do something, but don't get excited before the bear does. Unless you want to be the one to attempt to control the situation—leave this to the bear."

I moved off the trail to where I could see, and, lo and behold, there was Sterling bringing up the rear—ten teachers followed by a twelve-hundred-pound bear. Huge and well furred with many visible scars, he plodded slowly along, in a characteristic head-down, pigeon-toed walk.

Occasionally, and especially at McNeil River where bears and people share the same trails, bears will follow along at a polite distance behind a group. They do the same thing at Hallo Bay and Swikshak River in Katmai National Park and at Moraine Creek in Katmai National Park Preserve.

Do these bears want to be part of things and see us as entertainment, are they just curious, or are they just headed to the same place at the same time the people are? I'm uncertain.

Sometimes young bears continue following even if you stop,

approaching and displaying, as if wanting you to move. It's a stage they seem to quickly outgrow—kind of like the human "terrible twos."

But Sterling was no youngster.

Sterling had been a McNeil River bear for a long time. I'd observed him in encounters with Woofie a dozen years before. He appeared to be full-grown when I first saw him in 1991 and now, fifteen years later, he was *huge* and easily identifiable not only for his bulk but also for his two ears that no longer stood up. Fighting had uniformly broken cartilage until both ears were folded over, leaving him looking like a cross between a German shepherd and a Cocker Spaniel.

At McNeil, Sterling was considered to be a far-side bear. Not because Gary Larson is a folk hero at McNeil—he is—but rather because he always fished on the far or north side of the river where people aren't allowed and where the best fishing occurred. I can't ever remember seeing him on the south side. He almost always claimed what were likely the most productive fishing spots. In the ten years at McNeil, I never had any kind of interaction with him—he stayed on his side I and I stayed on mine.

He certainly wasn't on the far side now—only about fifty feet separated us.

When you are watching bears with me, the object is literally to *watch*, not to interfere or be an egocentric redneck Alaskan. John Muir said, "Any fool can destroy trees." Well, any fool can scare a bear. One object of the teacher training was to see bears being bears, so when Sterling kept on coming, I did what I always do—kept everyone together, whispered to them to stay quiet, and moved us slowly off the trail to a distance I hoped Sterling would be comfortable with. It worked and Sterling never gave any acknowledgment we were there. He never faced us, stopped, or exhibited any extraordinary behavior—unless one thinks, as I do, that an elderly bear walking close to a bunch of picture-taking humans is extraordinary. He passed by within twenty-five feet and disappeared up the trail toward camp.

I gave him ten minutes before following and proceeding on to the top of the stream and the lake where our camp was.

On this particular year the Alaska Department of Fish and Game had set up a fish weir for the purpose of counting every salmon that made it past the bears and commercial fishermen and into the lake to spawn. Made of vertically placed aluminum pipes, the weir resembled a pipe organ placed across the creek and made a barrier where water could flow but that salmon couldn't swim through or jump over.

Salmon had to stop their upstream migration until several pipes were lifted in the center, making a gate through which the fish could swim through one by one. Two fisheries technicians opened the gate and did their count when the fish numbers built up. The fish milling behind on the downstream side of the weir attracted three or four small bears, who evidently knew a good fishing spot when they got into one. The techs and bears coexisted, the techs staying on one side of the weir and the bears on the other.

When our group reached the weir, there was Sterling, chomping down on a freshly caught red salmon. There were no other bears in sight nor were there any others fishing for the four days Sterling occupied the weir site or rested on the bank above the stream. A few came by, but after spotting or smelling Sterling, they kept on moving and didn't try to fish. He was a mighty big bear.

We spent hours on the stream bank as Sterling fished and ate salmon not thirty feet away. He glanced in our direction from time to time and never bothered the weir guys, even when they took splashing fish out of the water to record weights and take scale samples.

Sterling used either front paw to fish. They were nearly a foot wide and he seldom missed a fish. Instead of chasing them through the shallows like the younger bears that had been at the weir, Sterling stood motionless until the fish came close, then he'd lunge, pinning the fish to the bottom with one of these huge front feet, then grab and hold with his teeth. He rarely missed.

Sometimes, when the creek was chock full of salmon, he'd modify his technique. He'd again stand still but would raise one foot slightly out of the water—looking like a hunting dog on point. When a salmon swam directly below his paw, he'd simply drop it down on the fish. Twelve-hundred pounds of weight and sharp front claws pinned the fish until he quickly removed it from the water using his impressive array of teeth.

One morning he was gone.

I would visit Tutuk Creek for fifteen more years but I never saw Sterling again. Maybe he liked the chum salmon that run up the McNeil at pretty much the same time the reds run up Tutuk ten miles to the north.

After dinner on the last night of our trip, we talked about what we had seen in the past five days. To a person the experience with Sterling stood out. His behavior and demeanor had changed everyone's attitude toward bears. No one wanted to forget the great brown bulk and massive head of Sterling as he slowly passed by, making his way to the Tutuk Lake.

Nothing particularly special happened that summer. A big old bear peacefully followed a group of humans as they walked along a trail, then let them watch him fish for four days.

But we were all changed.

# 28

## Safety in Bear Country

I have known people who have been killed by bears and people who have been severely mauled. You have read the stories. While we try to explain possible reasons for some incidents, we can only wonder why others occurred.

A poor choice of camping spots, like along bear trails in the middle of feeding areas or on the banks of salmon streams. Inadvertently coming into contact with bears defending moose and deer kills or even garbage cans. Startled mothers protecting against perceived threats to cubs. There is a long list of what can cause a bear to actually make contact with a person.

One day I sat on my favorite rock next to Tutuk Creek. Fishing nearby were Solstice and her two yearlings. All the other bears kept their distance as she or the cubs gave short bluffing rushes to any that ventured near.

Apparently, a subadult male wandered a little too close, perhaps more intent on salmon than keeping a respectful distance from the Queen of Tutuk Creek. With absolutely no warning, instead of breaking off her short charge, she broke into a run and grabbed the subadult from behind as he tried to flee from a bear more than twice his size. In a split second, she dragged him down in a brutal attack, biting him repeatedly. As quickly as she started, she stopped and returned to her cubs and her fishing spot. The poor subadult simply stood there bleeding and looking traumatized.

The moral of the story is this: Solstice began a physical attack instantaneously. If the other bear had been a person, the attack likely would have been fatal.

There is little doubt as the wild land–urban interface increases, more and more tragedies will occur. Mountain bike races, ultramarathons, adventure tourism, sport fishing, subdivisions in prime bear habitat, backcountry lodges—the list is endless, and all of these mean more contact between bears and people.

As I mentioned in chapter 25, in 2000 I wrote a booklet for the Alaska State Office of the National Audubon Society. *Living in Harmony with Bears* was designed to help people coexist with black, brown, and polar bears. The project was supported and approved by the Alaska Department of Fish and Game, National Park Service, U.S. Fish and Wildlife Service, U.S. Forest Service, and several conservation organizations. The booklet was widely circulated in Alaska and elsewhere and is still available on ADF&G, Audubon, and NPS websites. It has been translated into both Japanese and Russian.

In the chapter titled "Safety in Bear Country," I started with this premise: "Sometimes in spite of our good intentions we have unwanted encounters with bears."

The following sections are taken from the booklet. I annotated those sections here with further information and discussion.

BE PREPARED.

Plan how you are going to react when you meet an inquisitive, intelligent, and potentially dangerous animal in the backcountry—or in your neighborhood.

BE PREDICTABLE.

Many bears in Alaska have had interactions with people. As our population increases, this number will grow. What a bear learns in one encounter influences what it does in the next. Try to make every encounter positive—for you and the bear. If we want bears to be nonthreatening and predictable, it is important that we reciprocate.

BE CAREFUL.

Bears don't like to be surprised. If you are hiking in a place where you can't see, make your presence known by talking or clapping your hands.

A bear doesn't like to be surprised any more by you than it does by other bears. When you can't see and you don't wish to have an altercation, "Hey bear, ho bear" works, as does "Ho bear, hey bear."

Bears usually respond to hand claps by moving away. Perhaps this is because they don't clap much or more likely it is a sound they haven't experienced. However, I did see the female bear Fossey, named after Dian Fossey, of course, bring her forepaws together when apparently stressed, in quiet claps.

TRAVEL WITH A GROUP [or at least with a friend].

While this isn't always practical, the larger the group, the smaller the risk. Groups of people seem to intimidate bears. Bears are more likely to approach one or two people than larger groups.

MAKING EYE CONTACT WITH A BEAR IS UNLIKELY TO INFLUENCE THE BEAR OR TO AFFECT THE OUTCOME OF AN ENCOUNTER.

It is important to keep the bear in sight so you have the opportunity to detect visual clues to the bear's behavior.

KEEP CALM!!!!!!

If a bear approaches, keep calm. It is assessing the situation as it moves toward you. It's picking up clues as fast as you are giving them. If you get excited, the bear could too.

Do not escalate the situation. Let this be the bear's job. Your behavior should follow that of the bear. I am not certain where the idea of arm waving comes from, but certainly not from me. Ditto for looking big. It does help to stand up on something as it increases your confidence. If you are with a group, keep close together, and if you have a companion, stand shoulder to shoulder.

IDENTIFY YOURSELF AS A HUMAN AND DON'T RUN.

If a bear becomes increasingly stressed and aggressive, talk to it in a low voice. DON'T RUN. Bears can go about 35 mph—even the fat ones! [Usain Bolt tops out at 27.8.]

INCREASE YOUR DISTANCE.

Bears avoid antagonistic encounters by moving away from one another. If the bear is not moving toward you, very cautiously try to move away.

Increase your distance. Do this if you can. Nothing defuses an aggressive situation more.

IF A BEAR PERSISTS.

"Hold your ground."

If the bear keeps on coming and seems intent on causing you bodily harm, do whatever you think necessary to show the bear you are not intimidated.

MOST CHARGES STOP SHORT OF CONTACT IF YOU REACT APPROPRIATELY.

A head-down, open-mouthed, running charge is a bear's trump card. It is (almost assuredly) a defensive reaction to a perceived threat. The bear is telling you that it is highly stressed and you are in the wrong place. Charges can happen so quickly there isn't much time for reaction. A charge almost always ends short of contact.

DETERRENTS.

Pepper spray is a legitimate tool. However, due to misinformation it can give people a false sense of security. The effect of pepper spray in different situations is uncertain. . . . Pepper sprays are designed to be sprayed directly in a bear's face at close range.

Many commercial bear-viewing guides now carry handheld flares as well as pepper spray. There are numerous articles available on deterrents. Dr. Stephen Herrero, author of *Bear Attacks, Cause and Avoidance*, is the world's leading authority on bear-human interactions. His books, articles, and films are bibles for keeping both people and bears safe. My favorite quote of Steve's: "Pepper spray is not brains in a can." It isn't and shouldn't be confused with common sense. Safety in bear country is not rocket science.

Bear spray, signal flares, and large caliber handguns all have been shown to work in intimidating or killing bears, but in my fifty years with bears I have never had to use any of them.

Keeping a sharp lookout heightens one's enjoyment of the natural world. Get outside! Even if you don't see a bear, I promise you'll see many wonderful things.